AN ORDINARY GIRL'S GUIDE TO EXTRAORDINARY

AN ORDINARY GIRL'S GUIDE TO EXTRAORDINARY

the practical magic of finding
your awesomeness
(no matter who you are)

by Christy Shell

Copyright

The author of this book does not dispense psychological or health care advice, financial or medical advice, or prescribe the use of any information herein as a form of treatment for any situation or condition. The intent of the author is to offer information of a general nature and is intended only to educate and entertain you in your quest for a more fulfilling life experience. In the event you use any of the information in this book, the author and publisher assume no responsibility for your actions or results. If you need expertise, consult with the appropriate professional. This book does not contain all information available on the subject and has not been created to be specific to any individual's or organization's situation or needs. Every effort has been made to make this book as accurate as possible; however, there may be typographical and/or content errors. Therefore, this book should serve only as a general guide and not as the ultimate source of subject information.

Some names and details have been changed to protect the privacy of individuals. Brand and product names are trademarks of their respective owners.

ISBN: 978-0-692-06680-5

Printed in the United States of America

Zeal Coaching for Life & Career
3 E. Water Street
Troy, Ohio 45373

www.ZealCoach.com

To Mom and Dad. Your love got me here.
You are why I knew extraordinary was possible
to begin with.

Tell me, what is it you plan to do with your one precious and wild life?

- Mary Oliver

Contents

Introduction

Marie's Story

Marie is a beautiful young woman. If you met her, you might be a bit intimidated by her good looks and quiet confidence. She is intelligent, strong, quick with a smile, and charming.

For over 20 years, Marie has been the valued employee of a large retailer, rising from entry-level to the position of floor supervisor. She has been asked several times to join the company's corporate human resources team. Each time she turned down the offer.

Why? Because Marie is not who she seems, and yet, she is exactly who she seems.

Marie has been on her own since she was 16 when her father and brother were imprisoned for heinous crimes. With their conviction, she finally escaped the chaos and pain that had dominated her life for years. Marie has been making her own way ever since, determined to survive her struggles with other dysfunctional relationships and lots of self-loathing and shame.

During periods of relative calm, Marie would attend courses at the local community college where she did very well. Then the swirling drama of her family would suck her back in. During those times of chaos, Marie would lose her confidence and give up on her education.

Marie knew she could do better. She knew she wanted more from life. But she could not sustain enough forward motion to step into something better, like the HR position she repeatedly turned down.

Then something changed. Marie met a great guy. He saw who she was and who she wanted to become. Being fiercely independent and self-reliant, Marie was reluctant and suspicious, but he slowly won her over and gained her trust. His emotional support helped Marie sustain her strength and confidence. The tide began to turn in her favor. The day she first came to my office she had been married a few short months and was ready to start looking at what was possible for her life and career.

After several months of our working together, Marie began to acknowledge her gifts and talents and how they could uniquely serve the world. She came to realize she had value and that all her experiences, good and bad, happened for a reason. The wisdom she gained from those experiences was critical to understanding her purpose in life and deciding how she wanted to move forward.

Marie enrolled in the final classes to finish her degree and accepted the HR Manager position. Being in human resources was not her ultimate goal, but she took the job to gain experience and expand her confidence.

Through exercises during our coaching sessions, Marie began to see how she might help other women become financially stable, so they were not trapped in difficult circumstances. This was one struggle she had overcome, and Marie hated to watch other women have limited choices because of their lack of experience with money.

Now Marie's dream is to run a non-profit to help women overcome poverty, even if she must start it herself. She has been researching and learning all she can, finally graduating college with a degree in human services. Marie is on her way to making dreams happen for herself and for others who need her help.

Working with Marie and hundreds of other clients is the honor and the passion of my life. Guiding clients to discover and trust their unique purpose and natural wisdom transforms them and their lives. This evolution creates extraordinary results. Results that are unique to each person.

Every time it happens I am in awe of the magic of coaching and am profoundly blessed to be a witness to it.

That's what this book is about: this sweet journey, your sweet journey. The goal of this book is to share with you the fundamentals of how to navigate that journey, to uncover your sweet spot—the place where your passion, purpose, talents, and gifts intersect with the needs of the world. When you trust and act from your sweet spot, extraordinary things start happening. Extraordinary changes take place in you and in your world, no matter what your life has been like up to this point.

I am on a mission to transform the mindset of people who have stopped creating or expecting more for themselves and have decided to settle for ordinary. This book is a guide for the person who sees themselves as ordinary, and asks, "Why would anything awesome happen to me?" But deep inside continues to hold a glimmer of hope, that it will.

In short, this book introduces you to the steps it takes to transform your life from ordinary to extraordinary.

Yes, this is one of those books! The type that tells you that you can indeed create the awesome life you truly desire. It is even going to show you how to find and stay in the space where you can create things you never thought were possible, things you might even call miracles. It will share how my clients and I are taking our lives from ordinary to extraordinary, and how you can do the same.

But here is what this book will not tell you: it will not tell you that extraordinary happens overnight! It is not a "fix it once and done" process. Going from ordinary to extraordinary is a journey. It is an evolution. Changing your thinking and habits and creating results takes work, faith, and consistency, usually for years.

Becoming extraordinary is about knowing and accepting yourself and letting yourself shine, knowing you can be more. By rewiring your brain from the inside and the outside, you change your conscious thinking until your subconscious is altered and gets on board with this beautiful wild ride. Like mastering the piano or learning calculus—unless you are a musical prodigy, a mathematical genius or an enlightened guru—extraordinary doesn't come easily for most of us.

And there is this universal truth: you never actually arrive. You never "get there" because this is a journey and there is no finish line. There is no finale to extraordinary! Yes, you will overcome what seems like insurmountable obstacles to reach your goals, but there is always more to learn, to gain, and to give. The changes and growth continue until the end of your life.

I know it sounds exhausting but here is how it works. When you get aligned with yourself and the way of "being" outlined in this book, you worry less, and you love every day more. Not just the days you accomplish your goals, but every day. Your energy is focused on loving action, not on fear. Fear is exhausting. Loving action creates more energy. It is a renewable resource that you can tap into again and again.

So, when you get to your last day in this world, you will have had more days of joy and love, a positive impact on yourself, your family, and your community in small and miraculous ways. The world will be better because of how you lived and loved with your deeds and actions. That is real living. That is extraordinary.

Why Listen to Me?

It may occur to you to question why I am qualified to guide you on this journey. I am not famous, nor have I cured a single disease, not even a small one that just gives you a rash. But Marie's story is not so dissimilar to mine or even to yours. Maybe the details are different. Maybe you had a good or even a great upbringing, maybe your family supports and loves you, and you have all the resources you need to thrive. But there is a reason you picked up this book. Somewhere in your life or your career there is a level of dissatisfaction, some unrest, a sense that something is missing.

This need or yearning is universal. We all want meaning and purpose in our lives. Not just to maintain the status quo, but to experience deep satisfaction and to have an impact on the world. Not only to live an ordinary life but to be extraordinary.

I am here to shout it from the rooftops. It is possible for you, just as it has been possible for me.

I am an ordinary girl. If you could see me right now, you might see this soccer mom who has no relevance to you or to your life. But here's why you should listen to me. I was an unfortunate looking child, a nerd really. I came from humble beginnings. My mom and dad were divorced just after I was born. My mom was single and worked multiple jobs for many years before she married my stepfather. Both my mom and stepdad are orphans. I was a so-so student and didn't find out I had dyslexia until I was 29. My biological dad died when I was only 9 years old.

So my early family life was rough. I think for most people on some scale this is normal and even ordinary. I didn't really know we struggled because there were many positives. I always felt loved and cared for by both my parents and our large extended family. My parents were willing to work hard for a better life, to provide more advantages and opportunities for my brother and me.

In spite of the positives in my life, I made mistakes. I probably have a few more messes in my life than some people and less than others. So, yes I guess that makes me ordinary. I believe these mistakes made me stronger and clearer about who I truly am. They taught me compassion for other people's mess-ups and mistakes because I understand how they got to where they are.

My biological dad was a Marine when he passed away, and that gave me the opportunity to go to college for free. This one bittersweet gift changed my potential destination in life. My life could have gone down a completely different road, possibly a dark one. Sometimes that dark road looked easier, more fun. But, I chose—more often than not—to keep moving forward, to spiral up, to reach for extraordinary.

Looking back, I realize I learned my most valuable lessons from watching my mother's perspective on life—optimism, enthusiasm, compassion, and perseverance. She had the right mindset to succeed. Her example laid the groundwork for me to face my own obstacles, and have my own loving family. She inspired me to create my own success, running my own business and living a life far more extraordinary than I could ever have imagined.

Now I have the benefit of 20 years of education, both formal and informal self-study. I've invested in my own personal development and growth, being coached by mentors who understood my issues. Yes, I had to do my own work. Besides being coached, I have learned from my clients, soaking up every drop of knowledge and experience as I coached others. I have an innate, soulful knowing that life and career coaching are what I am meant to do. You too can gain this confidence about your career and life. I know because I have seen my client's lives completely transform. Often the seemingly impossible is made possible, through self-development, coaching, and the critical step called courageous action.

Purpose and Career

For some, finding your extraordinary purpose is about career selection. After all, you will spend 8 hours a day, for 250 days a year, for over 42 years working. That is 10,500 days or 84,000 hours of your life!

That is a lot of time if you haven't invested in finding your purpose. It is my hope that you will find something more profound here that will guide not only your career but your entire life, as well.

The most precious gift imaginable is your life. How do you want to spend your time, your precious energy, and your brainpower? You can default to something that will just pass the time, or you can actively choose something that is enjoyable and has meaning to you. Your choice might even help others or change humanity. It is entirely up to you.

You can view this insight as overwhelming and insurmountable, or you can see it as a call to action. I'm sure you can guess which road I favor. You have more than 10,500 days to impact the world in some positive and beautiful way. What road will you choose?

Louise's Story

Louise was a family friend back in my hometown, a lovely person who could light up a room with her smile. But I hadn't seen her smile in years except when talking about her adoring children, who were soon to leave the nest.

Louise had two issues she wanted to work through, figuring out her marriage and finding a career. For years I had suspected her husband of being a tyrant, and she confirmed this without many details except that it was worse than I had thought. Louise knew she needed to get out of her marriage, but she had no real education, no career prospects, and a debilitating fear of her future. Louise was capable of doing anything, but she was looking for something that would put her unique brand of free-spirit creativity, love of travel, and knack for connecting with seniors into her work.

We worked together for months to understand her fear, uncover her purpose and talents, and find careers that matched her talents. We helped her gain confidence, confirm that her marriage was not salvageable, dissolve her guilt about divorce, and figure out how to live on her own. When we took a short break, I was not sure what would happen. A few months turned into almost 11 months, and I wondered if any of our work had really taken.

Early during that 11-month time, Louise attended a fun group workshop at my office. *Envision 2015* was a dream board workshop that helped set goals and dreams for the coming year by creating a collage of photos and inspirational quotes. During the workshop, we didn't really get to talk, except I remember commenting on her board, "What if everything on there could come true?" She didn't respond to my comment, and I remember thinking that this stuff is hard, especially when you know what you want but it seems impossible to get there.

In the fall of that year, I got a message that Louise was desperate to see me. The day of our meeting, I was braced for the worst. When she arrived at my office her smile was like rock concert spotlights!! She was ecstatic. She said, "Everything came true!"

I know this may sound unbelievable, but this is how this stuff can work. Completely baffled, Louise proceeded to tell me that the month after she left her husband, she got two job offers that she hadn't even applied for. One was an interior designer's assistant, literally one of the things on her dream board. The second was a tour guide for senior citizen site-seeing tours across the country. You guessed it! Her dream board had photos of traveling and active older men and women. She took both jobs.

But here is the kicker. As if this wasn't enough, here's what Louise said next. "I completely blew you off that day. I actually threw my dream board in my trunk and didn't look at it for months. I remember working on it at the workshop, and being strangely connected, calm and excited all at the same time. When you made a comment about it coming true, I could not see how and dismissed you. Then a few days ago when I got the second job offer, I thought, 'Wait!' and I tore my house apart trying to find my board. When I remembered the trunk and opened it, I just sat down right on the garage floor and cried."

All I can say is this stuff is real. Now, I can't tell you how much my heart sings when Louise posts social media updates of her adventures with seniors all over the country! She will tell you through coaching and trusting the process, she allowed these things to happen in her life. She allowed her life to become her version of extraordinary.

Clearly, coaching changes lives and careers. Every moment you spend understanding and doing the work laid out in this book will reward you. I don't know how it will impact you specifically, that is between you and the Divine. I do know the work weaves its way through many different areas of your life including relationships, career satisfaction, and confidence. But your biggest gains will be in self-acceptance and a calm certainty. By learning to control the chaos in your mind, you allow your purpose and passions to run the show. And when that happens, everything in your life falls into place. Your version of extraordinary emerges.

Here is where we start.

Alignment and the Personal Trilogy

We all have three people who live inside of us. I call this concept your Personal Trilogy. These three individuals have different functions and different reasons for being there. When they're aligned, we're in a good place. When they're out of alignment—not so much!

Your Soul

The first person of the Trilogy we will call Soul. Soul is not necessarily connected to any religious faith. Actually, all faiths have a version of this concept of Soul, Spirit, Consciousness, or Karma.

Here I am generally referring to that magical part of you that you can't put your finger on, but you know is there. We are aware of it, we feel a sense of connection to it, and we know it is something bigger than ourselves. I don't care if you call it Soul, or God, or Divine, or the Grand Pooh-Bah, but religions and scientists for centuries have been trying to figure it out.

So I will keep it simple. Soul is the magical part that is there when you're born, and it leaves when you die. It's the light that turns on at birth and goes out when you pass away. It is here for a reason—to love and to experience being human. It also knows why you are here and what your unique contributions are.

When we are tuned in, we start to listen and to hear Soul's direction and wisdom. It's like an inner GPS saying, "Turn left in 400 feet." But the messages do not come in ways we have been traditionally taught, and learning a few simple techniques to connect to your Soul will help you decide how to do the "right" thing in many different areas of your life.

Your Person

The second person who forms a part of your Personal Trilogy is Your Person. This is literally your physical person and your personality—your biological self—which includes your brain and the hard wiring that forms your personality.

Your Person and its development determine the talents, skills, strengths, and physical attributes that are natural to you.

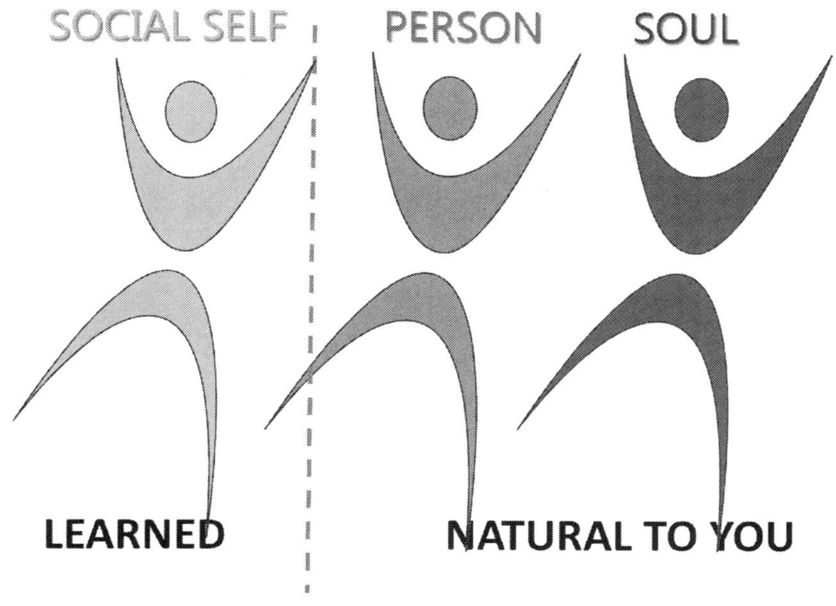

Your Social Self

The third person in the Trilogy is your Social Self. Your Social Self is everything you've learned since you were born. The first two parts of the Trilogy are natural to you, they were a part of the package when you were born. The third one is everything you've learned from family, church, media, friends—all the outside influences, how you make sense of them, and how they shape who you are.

If the Soul's purpose is to help you experience your purpose in life, the Social Self's mission is to help keep you safe. Think of all those lessons you were taught to keep you safe, to help you thrive, and to do things in ways acceptable to society as you grew up. Your Social Self is the judge that sets the rules you live by. It can be your greatest ally or your biggest bully.

Aligning the Trilogy

Imagine the three parts—your Soul, your Person, your Social Self—as paper dolls. If you stack them on top of each other and they line up nicely with no edges peeking out, you're happy and content because you're aligned or in alignment.

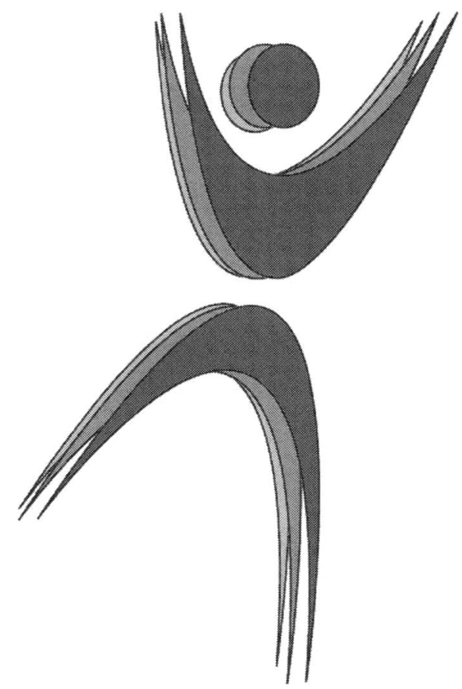

The More **Aligned** you are, the **HAPPIER** You Are.

When those paper dolls are stacked askew, you're out of alignment, prickly, out of sorts, and unhappy.

Say you're naturally very extroverted, which is one of the Person qualities, and your Social Self was taught to sit down and be quiet—maybe your parents hushed you all the time. Now that you're an adult, you're conflicted because you're naturally talkative, but there is always that little voice in your head telling you to be quiet. This is where the Social Self starts to pull you out of alignment, and you start thinking that there is something wrong with you because you can't be quiet.

Plus, because you have internalized that talking is wrong, you don't even consider a career in sales, teaching, or as the lead announcer for the World Wrestling Federation, where being a talkative extrovert is valued. Or you don't speak up in a meeting when you have an idea, nor do you talk to that attractive guy who lives across the hall, and you don't even think of complaining to the groomer who scalped your Golden Retriever and then over-charged you. Now, who is hushing you?

You can see how one misdirected thought or belief can pull you entirely off track.

In this process, we start by looking at your Soul and Your Person to understand who you are naturally at your core. Then we examine your Social Self—what it thinks and believes, and how harshly it may be judging you.

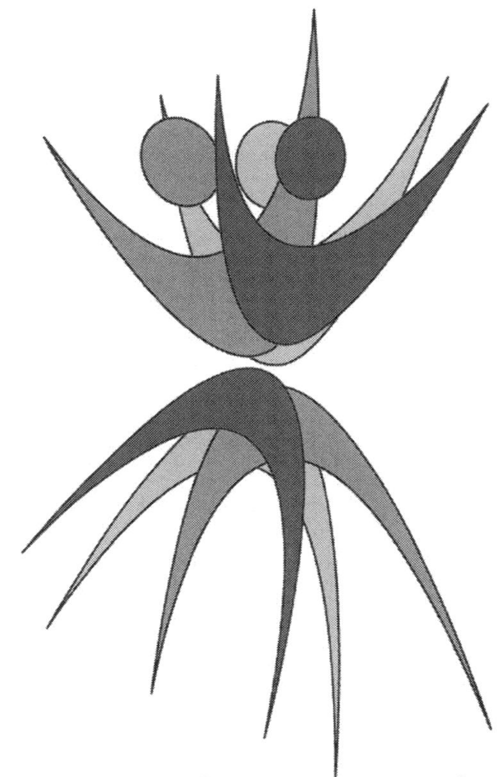

Misaligned is not very happy!

- Does your Social Self align with what your Soul and Your Person need?
- Where is it pulling you away from who your Soul and Your Person genuinely are?
- Do you even know who you are because your Social Self is so overbearing?

When all your parts are equal and in alignment with one another, you're happy.

When they're not aligned, you're not happy. How do we get the parts of your Trilogy nicely aligned? That's what we're going to figure out in this book.

Part 1: Starting with SOUL

The simple word "Soul" invokes many different feelings and reactions from people based on their upbringing and experience. These feelings usually fall into three categories:

1. a loving, warm connection

2. pain, guilt, and anger

3. indifference and disbelief

Many religions have truly damaged the Soul's reputation and potential power by turning people away with their fear-based tactics (a Social Self idea, by the way) while many others have saved lives with their love and service. These extremes leave us confused and sometimes at war with each other and within ourselves.

In this book, we are talking about the Soul in the simplest terms. The Soul is the magical and mysterious light (energy, consciousness, spirit) within each of us that comes when we are born and leaves when we die. We will never fully understand it while we are alive. The Soul is a part of God, the Divine, the "Force" and it connects us to more than ourselves. It connects us to all that is.

In even simpler terms, I like to describe it as "God is Love." This is how I explained God to my children when they were young: "Do you love me?" I would ask. "Yes," they would answer. That feeling of love is God. Love is simply what God is all about, being loving to yourself and to others.

Like a magnet, the Soul thrives on love and is attracted to love, like a flower is attracted to sunlight. We are naturally drawn to love, and we thrive in an atmosphere of love.

The Soul is who you are at your deepest level, your truest self. We think our personality or our physical body is who we are, but the Soul is the inner person, the inner knowing. It's your consciousness, it's the voice saying, "Isn't that interesting." It's the thinker inside you. It is the participant and the observer of your life. Its natural state is love, and that never changes.

When Fear Takes Over

But here is the problem: this simple, beautiful connection to your Soul, this way of living and being, gets lost in today's society. So many of us have lost or squelched that knowing, that natural and real connection to being lead by love and its wisdom. Why?

The answer is fear. Fear is the mortal enemy of love. If you really think about it, all "wrong" actions and bad decisions come from fear: fear of not having enough, fear of not being enough, fear of being alone, fear of being wrong, and fear of being judged. We create countless fears for ourselves. Stealing, lying, cheating, manipulating, betrayal, hating—all start with fear. Why does a child start to lie? Because she is afraid she will get into trouble, so she learns to lie in an attempt to keep herself out of trouble.

When we are born, we are only afraid of two things: falling and loud noises. Everything else we fear is something we were taught or something we deduced from our experiences. The key thing to know now is how all these fears sabotage our ability to focus on love and its messages. We must discern, when we are making decisions, whether they are guided by fear or by love, and that is really the key. When you can listen to your Soul from a loving mentality and connection, it will guide you to the most extraordinary places.

The Heart of Soul

You are to the Divine like a single drop of water is to the ocean. The Divine, like water, runs through all things, including you. Water is naturally drawn to water. Love is naturally drawn to love.

Doubt is Fine

Accepting or even entertaining the notion that the above is true will give you a clearer understanding of why it is essential to explore your Personal Trilogy. If you find yourself skeptical or reserving judgment, that is completely fine too. If you already believe and live this way, that is fantastic.

Here's the thing, you don't have to believe with a capital B. I'm not trying to convert you to any one faith. But unless you have some understanding of this concept, it's hard to connect to the fire inside you. When your purpose is not connected to something bigger it always feels a little hollow.

For example, your goal can be to bake bread, but unless you there is a deeper purpose behind that goal—perhaps wanting to feed and nourish people—your goal will feel hollow, like so much busywork. You might want to build homes, and that could feel empty, but if you're going to build homes for families to be warm and safe, that feels very different on a Soul level. This is where your goals become a meaningful mission, and love is a critical part of that meaning.

You don't even have to believe this concept of the Divine or Soul because this force is working for you whether or not you believe in it. You don't have to be connected to God, nor do you have to dwell on the concept of God. You can do things out of kindness rather than out of fear, or you can do them from a place of giving. I personally believe God is trying to connect with you in any way he can. So, if you're doing good things, he's with you. If that turns you off at this point in the book, I would just ask you to hold that thought and keep reading.

As long as you're not resisting, this process can work for you.

Learning How to Listen: Your Internal GPS

Your Soul is always naturally communicating with you and guiding you. It does this throughout your daily life. Like an internal Global Positioning System (GPS), it is always giving you direction. All you have to do is turn it on and listen. It "speaks" to you through your physical feelings, natural instincts, intuitions, and desires. Your Soul guides you toward things that bring you joy and light you up, and it steers you away from things that feel heavy, weigh you down, and feel icky or wrong for you.

To tune into your internal GPS, the first step is to develop a baseline of understanding what you're attracted to and what you're naturally good at, and conversely, what turns you off or repulses you.

- What are you passionate about?
- What do you crave to create, experience, or feel?
- What makes you feel trapped?
- What is a complete turn off?

These reactions are your Soul communicating with you. It is that simple. This is intuition, but most people have disregarded their intuition for so long they don't even know it works, never mind how to listen to it and interpret its messages.

If this is you, don't worry, one of three things is probably happening:

1. You are caught in the cycle of pleasing others and living their expectations of you, and in that process, you have lost sight of your unique gift to the world.
2. You are already living your purpose and don't recognize it. Maybe you got so driven to accomplish it that you lost sight of why.
3. You have never stopped to think about it. Maybe you didn't even know it was an option for you.

Regardless, the first steps to uncovering your purpose are to slow down, get introspective, and ask for help. Through quiet reflection and deciding to be open to insight and learning, you are opening up your GPS airways.

Once you have adopted this frame of mind, I

suggest you ask for clarity. You can do this with a prayer or meditation, or while you're scrubbing your feet in the shower—it doesn't have to be complicated. Simply ask the Divine or your great-whatever, "Please show me what my purpose is. I am open to knowing." Then stand by and listen. It's that easy—you have just turned on your internal GPS system.

Why do we ask the Divine for help? I am a firm believer that in every situation you have free will. You are 100% responsible for your life. But paradoxically, I also believe that you have a purpose and your Soul, the Divine part of you, already knows what that purpose is. So why wouldn't you ask for guidance?

The Divine has the perfect plan for you, often a better fit than you can create for yourself. When you adopt the idea that you are co-creating your life with the Divine like an equal partnership, that is powerful. Then the question becomes "Are you going to enlist your powerful partner for help or not?"

Looking Backwards for Evidence

One way to start becoming aware of how your guidance system has already been working in your life is to think about past experiences where you acted on instinct, and the results were better than you imagined. It could be how you met your partner or found a great job. Here's an example of how this happened in my life before I was aware of consciously connecting with my guidance system.

When I was a junior in high school, my closest friends included the class salutatorian as well as other kids whose parents were either physicians or executives. I was hanging out with the smart kids. Not necessarily the popular kids, but the smart kids. When invitations came around to go on a trip as a student ambassador to Europe for the summer, all my close friends got an invitation. The intent was to invite the kids who could afford it and were smart. I wasn't wealthy or in the National Honor Society, but I wanted to go. I didn't know why. I think it was about the adventure and not being left out, but I *really* wanted to go. I also knew that it was more than a whim. I felt compelled.

It was not like me to take the initiative, but I started to do some snooping. I found out that you didn't necessarily have to be invited and that students could ask to go. So I took a risk. I sat my mom and my stepdad down and said, "I really want to go on this trip," then went on to explain all the reasons why and how they didn't have to pay a cent. I had a small amount of money my biological dad had left for me and wanted to use that money for the trip.

My parents decided to allow me to go—and that was a very big deal. Just the act of asking transformed me, because it was the first time I took control and made something happen. I learned that I can be confident and bold and that well thought-out risks can pay off.

Visiting six different countries changed my 16-year-old perspective. I discovered that I was a world citizen, while at the same time it increased my pride in being an American. One of the most intriguing aspects of the tour was getting to visit Russia in the Soviet Union, still a communist country in 1985. At the time Americans did not get to see Russia even on TV. I just could not get over that our Cold War enemy was a vast country living 20 years behind us. It was literally like stepping back into the late 1950s and early 1960s. It was the one part of our trip that I could not stop thinking and talking about.

Later when I decided on my college major in Outdoor Recreation and Park Administration, my only goal was to be a summer camp director. Summer camp is where I first blossomed and felt accepted. It went right along with my love of the outdoors and helping people, specifically kids, to gain confidence and open themselves up to new experiences.

Three years later a professor in one of my classes started talking about looking for a group of students to live and work in the American Embassy in Moscow. The team would be required to run a summer camp for the kids associated with the US Embassy. Of course I knew it was my destiny!

I spent nearly four months in Moscow having some of the most improbable experiences of my life. Communism fell the summer after I had been there and I felt oddly honored that I got to witness the country before that happened. The impact that experience has had on my life is immeasurable, all because I listened to my guidance system and followed my instinct and desire to travel.

Now it is your turn. Not everyone will have a story with such clear connections, but if you look at some of the best times of your life, you will find clues.

- What were you doing?
- Who were you with?
- How did you behave?
- What was the purpose?
- What parts did you especially enjoy?
- Why did you enjoy it?
- What was the most meaningful part of the experience for you?

This is critical information that will show you already know how to follow your instincts—your internal GPS.

Body Compass

One of the most dependable and straightforward ways of deepening your ability to hear and follow your instinct is to use your body to tune in to the messages. The essence of this concept is that Soul uses your body to communicate with you.

I think of it this way. Your Soul lives in the same space as your body, kind of all smashed up in there with your physical organs like an overstuffed suitcase. So the most natural way the Soul has to communicate is by directly speaking to your body, through physical sensations.

Now you might believe the brain is the part of your body that communicates with you and guides you. That's a common belief, and there is some truth to it. However, though we may think our brain knows best, that's not true. The brain is more like a computer, and it believes whatever it is programmed to believe. The brain is essentially the Social Self. It uses past experiences to make decisions, and it also likes to follow whatever is new and exciting. That can lead to all kinds of confusion when you're trying to find your purpose in life because your Soul and not your brain, is your truest self.

Here is how the Body Compass works. Say someone walks into the room, your stomach tightens, and you feel an instant distrust of that person. That is your Soul speaking to your body (the tightening), which then signals your brain to register the information. The brain translates that feeling in your body into words. The sensation in your body is the Soul's way of communicating with you. The trick is to be aware of what your body is feeling, as that puts you in touch with what your Soul is trying to tell you. The first step to understanding how this works is to calmly notice what you're feeling in your body at any given moment.

Here's an example of the difference between body and brain. Imagine you are blindfolded and there are an orange and an apple on the table in front of you. You pick up each fruit and recognize them by touch and smell. Which one do you prefer?

If you have the thought, "Orange is better because it has vitamin C," or "The apple is better because it has good fiber," that's your brain talking. If you choose based on which scent is more enticing to you, or which one makes your mouth water, that is your body reacting to its preference for the orange or the apple.

You can apply this logic to any situation. Sometimes I wake up craving the outdoors or being near a body of water. That's not my brain thinking, "I need to be outside, outside is good for me." It's my body yearning for something that my Soul needs to thrive.

So when I am coaching a client about their career direction or a decision they need to make, I ask questions, and I watch for signs of their body reacting. It's like a version of the childhood game, *Hot & Cold*. In this game, there are degrees of closeness to the prize, as your partner gives you clues of "warmer, colder, hotter," etc. The "hotter" the feedback you get the closer you are to the prize. Here are some questions to ask to tune into your body compass:

- Does something feel good?
- Bad?
- Better or worse?
- Heavy or Light?
- Icky or wonderful?

It helps to establish guidelines for your body's physical reactions. Remember how you felt the first time you fell in love? Did you feel butterflies in your stomach or goosebumps? Did the hair on your arms stand up? What physical sensations do you feel when you meet someone you instantly like or dislike? Those are your body's reactions, or "Soul Quakes." Notice them and begin to play the Hot & Cold game using your Soul Quakes as indicators.

Robert's Story

I received a frustrated call from a mom one afternoon. Her son, Robert, was flunking out of college and partying like he was being paid for it. She wanted to know if I could help. With no promises, I offered to see him and try to figure out what was going on.

In my opinion, everyone wants to do well in life. When they are not thriving, it is an indirect call for help. The challenge is to discover whether that person wants help and if they are willing to try something different to help themselves.

Robert reluctantly kept his appointment with me. When he arrived, he looked like he just woke up from the fraternity party room floor. He didn't belong to a fraternity, but you get the picture. As we started getting to know each other, I asked him what his major in school was.

"Computers," he replied.

"Oh, what part of computers do you like?" I asked.

"I actually really hate it," he replied.

"So why did you decide to study computers?" I asked.

"I knew there were a lot of jobs and I could make a lot of money," he responded.

If you don't recognize Robert's answer as a red flag with warning alarms blaring, I implore you to keep reading. That was the first clue I uncovered in our initial meeting. The best thing about that conversation was that he knew he was in trouble and he wanted help.

Over the next few months, I discovered the real issue. Robert had been a star baseball player who didn't get much guidance in high school about getting recruited for college ball. When his dream of playing at the college level didn't materialize, he was deeply devastated and started partying to mask that pain and still be considered "cool." He was so committed to partying that he was enrolled at the state college in our town but lived at the private university because they had better parties. As I said, he was partying like it was his job and he was being paid for it. He had just shortened his commute to "work."

I also discovered Robert was fascinated with money and how it worked in business. He liked the idea of making money. This was not a shallow desire for him. It was a real curiosity.

One day in our session we were playing *Hot & Cold* to generate ideas for the different directions he might explore. I was offering him different blends of possibilities that might suit him to see what he thought, but more importantly, to see how he physically reacted.

Me: "Baseball coach?"

"Warm," he replied.

Me: "A sports journalist?"

"Warm," he replied.

Me: "A sports agent?"

"Warmer," he replied.

Me: "CFO for the Cincinnati Reds?"

His whole body reacted with a startled flinch, and a huge smile spread across his face with dimples like I had never seen! It makes me smile, thinking about it right now. That is what we call a Soul quake. He loved that CFO idea so much, his body could do nothing but react. We were onto something. This one conversation opened up some clarity about what his ultimate dream might be. It gave him hope.

Robert changed his major to Finance. He slowed down the partying. He explored walking on the college team (getting on a team without being recruited) but found it was not possible that late in his college career. He did join the college club team for a season but decided he just liked playing in a recreational league with his friends. He made peace with baseball and still goes to every game he can. He plans to coach someday when he has kids.

Robert called me last year to invite me to lunch.

He had graduated and is now a budding investment advisor. I could not stop staring when he arrived in a gorgeous suit and tie. I never realized how tall he was before. It was a case of the ugly duckling turned into a suave swan. It was terrific to hear how well he was doing. But more than anything, I could tell he had real pride in himself, almost as much as the pride I felt for what he had achieved.

- So what lights you up?
- What makes your Soul quake?
- What if you only did the things that made you feel alive or "hot?"
- What if you only did things that woke up your Soul?
- How would your life be different?

These answers will get you closer and closer to your purpose. One key is to keep trying new and different things you're curious about. Then as you have these new experiences, scan your body. Do you love it? Cold? Warm? Hot? Keep exploring until you get to red hot, your body literally buzzes, and you feel compelled to continue.

Resource: You can find the link to download a workbook containing these questions at the end of the book.

Other Ways to Listen to Soul

There are many ways the Soul communicates with us. Some people get information through dreams. Others meditate or sit quietly, taking the time to be still and open to connecting. I find the space between sleeping and waking to be a time when I'm open to receiving guidance.

Many people feel Soul connection in a community or their church. Being in nature is another way to connect. Music is one of the most common forms of connecting that everyone can relate to. Communicating doesn't always have to be serious. Play, laughter, and dancing are other ways to access messages from the Divine.

Sometimes people get messages from other people. I call these "Legacy Statements." This has happened to me several times over the years. One example is with this book. I was telling my website designer, who is also a dear friend and life coach, about the Personal Trilogy concept. She said, "Christy, that is a book!" And to be truthful, a huge cuss word involuntarily came out of my mouth. "F*%K, I can't write a book!"

You may recall I have mild dyslexia! Dyslexia is a learning disability that affects reading comprehension, spelling, and writing. So writing anything is challenging for me, to say the least.

It took going into hand-to-hand battle with my Social Self gremlins, but here I am, writing a book.

My friend's comment was a Legacy Statement. I know because as I was cussing, my whole body was tingling—Soul quake on speed!

The number one indicator to test the truth of any communication is by noticing how it feels in your body.

- Does it resonate with you?
- Does it feel like the truth?
- Notice the severity of your reaction.
- Does it invoke excited fear?
- Does your stomach do a flip-flop?

Your body knows the truth. And it willingly shares that knowledge when you listen closely.

From Soul Quakes to Soul's Goal

Your Soul is here to have a human experience: to grow, learn and serve in a way that is unique to you and helps the world. Your single most critical task as a human being is to discover your reason for being alive, your Soul's goal. It is to figure out how or what you are here to do, to experience, to love, to change, to be. By practicing and utilizing your body compass and noting what experiences and thoughts bring on Soul quakes, you will start to get indicators that will lead to your Soul's goal.

Remember, the one big over-arching reason your Soul is here is to learn how to love more deeply. To learn to love—or to contribute to—the world from your essence, from the most genuine part of you, requires that you turn that contribution into something real and practical that has an impact– large or small.

Your Soul's Goal or your purpose is not necessarily a lofty one like eradicating poverty or cancer, or whatever we have decided is a noble goal for society. Purpose can be simple and straightforward, practical or idealistic.

Look at the client examples I have already illustrated in this book:

- Marie's Soul goal is to help women learn about money so they can be independent.
- Louise's Soul goal is to be loving and creative by showing seniors the world.
- Robert's Soul goal is to help people invest their hard-earned money so they can have security and prosperity. And he wants to have fun while doing it.

My husband's mission is to solve complex problems. As a manufacturing engineer, his problem solving often serves a larger purpose that might not be readily apparent. Nevertheless, he thrives on applying his know-how to arrive at solutions that make contributions to a larger outcome. As much as reading this will make him cringe, he loves the world through his problem-solving. The Soul's goal does not have to be any more elaborate or world-changing than that.

This became apparent recently when one of his company's essential plants was hit by a tornado, shutting down the entire production facility. Guess who they called to get the production back online and replace all the machines destroyed in the storm? Now it was all hands on deck to get everyone working again, and Stev was a critical leader in accomplishing that. Talk about complex problem-solving. Like a rock star, in record time they are back up and running. His purpose got people back to work just weeks before Christmas.

My Soul's goal has evolved over the years. When I was young it was simple: to help people love and grow. That overall theme has not changed, but the focus and the language have. I adjust it as needed to feel inspired and connected to it. Until recently, the goal was "igniting lives with passion, purpose, love, and success." We still use this version as the tagline for my business. Then just a year ago, while I was doing a free-writing exercise for my business I clearly got a new message when I wrote, "I help Souls come out to play." This is my current Soul's goal.

Your Turn: Finding Your Soul's Goal

So how do you identify your Soul's goal? You dream. Play with intentional dreaming questions starting with "What if…?" Then insert your desire, something you know you want. Find a simple way to express your hope or dream. For example:

- What if I could help kids get adopted?

- Why is that important to me?
- Why is (that answer) important to me?

Keep asking questions until you find your underlying and most accurate reason for wanting to help kids get adopted.

This process helps to weed out options that sound nice but are not really important to you. When that's the case, the answers all kind of fizzle out and don't spark any fire for you.

Some people find their Soul's goal by getting still and quiet—like in a meditative state, relaxed and open. In that place, they ask questions similar to those in the example above or those listed below.

I get my answers when I'm on the move—walking in nature, on the water kayaking, driving in the car, or as I said before, in that time between being asleep and awake in the morning. I do notice I need to be alone when looking for my answers. I generally ask the Divine a question, and then I just continue my walk, enjoying nature or my dogs. The answer usually comes when I stop worrying about getting an answer, when I am just being in the moment.

The key is to figure out when you seem most connected to the Divine.

Sometimes the Divine has a sense of humor, and the answer comes in a lightning bolt. Well not literally, but the answer comes seemingly out of nowhere, quick and clear!

Here are a few questions to help you.

- What do you desire most in life?
- What makes you feel most alive?
- What compels you to take action?
- What do you daydream or night dream about most often?
- How would you like to impact or contribute to the world?
- What problem would you like to solve?
- What do you think, if changed, would make the world be a better place?
- What injustice or stupidity makes you angry?
- What are you jealous or envious of that other people have in their life?
- What gets you up in the morning?
- What holds your attention or your imagination?
- What are you pretending not to know about yourself, that you offer the world?
- What are your dreams for your life this year, in 10 years, 30 years and when you grow old?
- What do you want to experience and feel?
- What is the one impossible dream that you may be too embarrassed to tell anyone about?

Now go get a piece of paper, a journal, even a chisel and stone tablet—I don't care. But you must write these answers down, so you can look at them, add to them, change them, and feel them to see what resonates with you and has staying power.

Does the dream still seem charged with energy every time you think about it? Or was the idea a passing one?

It's critical to not judge your answers. Do not judge whether they are possible or impossible, silly or important. Also, don't judge yourself about whether you are capable, smart, or worthy enough. Don't worry about the "right" answer. Then look at all the answers and ask yourself this one last question.

What is my Soul in the world to do?

It may be simple, so simple you'll wonder if that is really it. You will know because you will feel a quiet and excited—maybe even electric—knowing along with peace and contentment.

Just dream. Please. It will get you there.

This process may take time, or it may happen right away. But your Soul knows. Allow it space, patience, and kindness to help it ease out of hiding.

Once you're clear about it, knowing your particular purpose gives you direction and meaning. It gives you a reason to move forward and a way to pursue things. Purpose permeates your life, across time and circumstance, at all ages. You'll have different roles to play during your life, but within those roles—child, student, parent, employee, manager, grandparent—there is one continuous theme or reason that usually carries through.

The Soul, being your most genuine self, is the foundation that your Personal Trilogy aligns to, so gaining clarity here is instrumental in finding the extraordinary life that you have at your fingertips.

An Extraordinary Story

There is this unremarkable area of green space that sits in the middle of our tiny town. New Bremen, Ohio, population circa 3000, is the home of a large family-owned company and it's where my husband works. We are not from New Bremen, we are transplants. This is an essential element of this story. If you have ever lived in a small town you know when you are not "from" a small town that really means you barely belong there. My mind didn't care about being from there or not, when I started dreaming about a green space, literally dreaming about a place where I barely belonged.

Dreaming about grass doesn't seem at all extraordinary, but it was. I was dreaming about what that green space could be. This area was already a quiet sleepy park, usually used once a year as part of the town festival. The rest of the year people walked around this space and during lunchtime workers would sit in their cars facing it. I couldn't stop thinking about it.

The best I could discern from the dream, it would be an "art park," a park with interactive art pieces.

And there was more, it would be the village green, the heart of the town. A place for families to gather to play, listen to music, and a place for employees to have lunch outdoors.

The craziest thing is I could see it in my mind's eye. I started drawing it. I blew up Pinterest collecting unique park design photos and interactive art examples, like "The Bean" in Chicago. I started talking about it to my family. That was met with little smirks and shakes of their heads at me. I was not offended by their reactions because like the boy who cried wolf, I love to think up new ideas, but I don't usually do anything about them. But this dream park was different. I wanted to make it happen! I was obsessed.

Then the tree came down. I love trees, so it is not surprising that this was a catalyst for me. It wasn't until a vast cottonwood growing in the green space was chopped down that I realized part of the green space was slated to become a parking lot for a new office being built adjacent to it. My heart stopped. They were turning my dream into a parking lot! This can't be happening. I could not let this happen. It was the moment of decision — to take action or let it go.

So I took a risk, a risk that I would be completely dismissed. Or worse, laughed at. I called the mayor. I told him I had an idea and asked if I could meet with him. To my shock, he said yes. I really didn't think this meeting was going to go anywhere, so I prepared a very informal presentation with my pictures from Pinterest. When I arrived at his office for the meeting, he pulled the city manager and the economic development director into the meeting. Yikes! With a deep breath and a here-it-goes-attitude, I shared my crazy dream.

They actually loved the idea! But the mayor requested I be patient for six to twelve months while the town finished several construction projects including that parking lot before having another conversation. He assured me that even with the parking lot, there was still enough room for my idea. Disappointed and looking for commiseration, I told a few close friends about my plan and the meeting.

Two weeks later, the economic director asked me to meet her for coffee. She shared that there was a state grant that fit my idea perfectly. The only catch was it had to be done in eleven days. I already had an over-scheduled workload, and the dyslexia issue loomed large in my head. Eleven days! I didn't think it was possible. At that moment one of the friends I had been commiserating with walked up and enthusiastically committed to writing the grant. Again, I can't make this stuff up!

This park seemed destined to be. During our last-minute presentation to the town council asking for permission to pursue the grant, we received a unanimous "Yes" vote!

Two months later, we received the grant, but it was

only a portion of the money we needed. Miraculously, we quickly found a benefactor, a woman who owns the bank in our town and was the last generation of her family. The park would become her family's legacy. The meaning just kept piling on. We soon had a purpose-driven committee to make the park happen. My dream was now the dream of many people.

I can't lie, there were lots of bumps in the road. Some we thought would stop the dream in its tracks, but we didn't give up. The amount of time and attention everyone put in was baffling. But in the spring of 2017, 4 1/2 years after that first meeting, the Komminsk Legacy Park was completed and dedicated. With the committee, the village employees, and the generosity of our benefactor, the park became more than I ever imagined it could be with a performance area, playable water feature, all-weather musical instruments, and more.

Ironically in a bittersweet decision for my family, we moved away a few years ago. And the committee made up of those friends I commiserated with, took complete loving ownership. It is not my park, it never was. Yes, it came to me in my dream, but it was a gift from the Divine. You would believe this too if you could see the families gathering and playing there now. I tear up every time I visit and see cute three-year-olds dancing in the fountain in their drooping, soaked tutus and grandparents playing musical instruments while grandchildren laugh with delight.

It is made from love. It offers love, and that is why it happened. It is pretty extraordinary!

This is just one example of what happens when you follow your Soul's messages. Notice how I got confirmation along the way, when people just started to show up to help unexpectedly and things started to fall into place. These were nods from the Divine that we were on the right track. Notice also that I was open to "allowing" it to happen in the way it needed to evolve. I was not forcing it to be my way or nothing. I literally reminded myself and my committee often that it was not our park, it was the community's park. We were just the hands assigned to the task of turning it from a dream into reality.

Finally, we kept connecting to the meaning and the reason why we were doing it: to create a heart for the community, out of love. And that is exactly what happened. My Soul's goal of letting Souls out to play incarnated as the Komminsk Legacy Park.

Part 2: Your PERSON

Going back to the concept of three people living inside you, let's look at the second one, which I call "Your Person." This is the part we generally think of as "me." It is your physical body and all the attributes of your personality. It's the biology of who you are and how you were hardwired when you were born; your character, disposition, skills, interests, and physical qualities. These traits reveal another part of you and how you interact with and move through the world.

Your Person is the physical biology and the nature of your personality that you were born with. These characteristics are natural to you. Depending on how you were raised or programmed as a child, you might act authentically and in tune with these traits, or you might be continually fighting them and experiencing the resulting stress.

Your Person is needed and necessary. It was created as the vehicle for your Soul's mission, to work through your body, to learn, and to accomplish what your Soul needs to do. Your Person is unique and specific to you, to your purpose, and to your journey. Never again in history will there be another person just like you. Your Person, along with your Soul, is what makes you and every other person genuinely unique. These natural traits are the best gift we have to give the world.

Generally, when we use our natural abilities, we enjoy life more. Using our natural talents feels good—not just because we are good at them, but also because they are fun to do. Knowing, developing, and mastering these abilities helps to formulate the Soul's goal into a career or way of living that is aligned with our natural self. So taking some time to discover and acknowledge Your Person builds your self-awareness and allows you to hone your life experience towards gaining satisfaction and bringing your highest value to others.

The simplest way for me to explain this is by looking at an example in nature, specifically, the duck!

Duck Theory

The duck has a small head, wide body, crazy skinny legs, and flat rubbery feet. Ducks are the funniest animal ever. Their parts don't look like they go together, but ducks are talented. They can waddle around on land. They can swim and fly, even dive underwater in search of food. They have the strangest collection of natural abilities, skills, and talents.

Blended together, the duck's attributes culminate in some incredible abilities. The duck has its own internal guidance system allowing it to fly all over the world. It can handle extremes of cold and heat, raising its young on every continent except Antarctica, and it can swim underwater without getting wet. The duck is perfectly engineered for what it does in the world.

But here's the thing: it doesn't know it's a duck. It just lives and breathes and does its amazing duck thing.

The same goes for you. Generally, we humans are wandering around just being who we are, without seeing that we are perfectly engineered for specific things. Unaware of what makes you uniquely you, like the duck, your inner GPS is communicating with you, but you're so busy trying to survive and fit into your environment that you can't see the unique combination of traits that make you ideally suited for your purpose.

As humans our trouble is, we too often don't recognize or stop and listen to our instincts, or even worse we write off our natural skills as nothing special or valuable. We take our unique, wonderful, and possibly strange collection of attributes for granted.

If a duck doesn't even know it's a duck, how are you supposed to automatically know who you are? You have to take steps to understand yourself rather than just wandering around hoping to discover the right path by accident.

Begin by Releasing Judgment

If you stood in front of the mirror right now what would you see? If you let go of all your thoughts about being pretty or ugly, thin or fat, smart or dumb, and you just looked without judgment—no good or bad—what would you see? This is incredibly difficult for most people… to see themselves without judgment.

When you start to dig in to uncover Your Person, you need to be objective, so you can actually see what you're looking for. We too often discredit our gifts or judge them as good or bad. These habits of thinking are Social Self messages, not true to our natural self. To explore Your Person, you need to adopt an "Isn't that interesting" frame of mind, to understand without judgment.

- Isn't that interesting; I picked up that new rhythm before my friends?
- Isn't that interesting; my teacher asked me to tutor another student in French?

- Isn't that interesting; my kids know our dinner is ready when the smoke alarm goes off?

Attributes are just attributes. They are not bad. They are not wrong. They give us information about ourselves. The ability to notice and utilize this information is critical. Doing so gives us a new perspective on how these attributes may be useful and even valuable resources to the world.

The lack of a particular skill is useful information too, not to be judged harshly. We spend so much time belittling ourselves for not being able to do something. We waste precious time and energy on improving our weaknesses instead of focusing on our natural raw talents and developing them into real skills.

Don't get me wrong, you can learn to do most anything if you really dedicate yourself, but eventually, you will hit a learning wall that becomes a roadblock to mastery and genuine contribution. Remember you are strongest when you are co-creating with the Divine, and that process is grounded in your natural-born talents. They are clues to your purpose, and to the differences you can make. So embrace your natural skills and see them for the resources they are on your journey.

Releasing judgment also helps you to explore the entire gamut of possibilities. You have probably come to know many of your natural qualities, mostly because you needed or used them often. Others may have been recognized or even criticized by others.

Jealousy from others—often masked as criticism—can be a good indicator that you have something unique and special.

You may also have critical skills you aren't aware of. Some are hidden to you because of lack of opportunity or the need to uncover them. Like mining for gold, we need to keep digging and discovering through new experiences. Grandma Moses, the world-renowned American painter, didn't start painting until she was 78.

Many attributes of Your Person are hidden in plain sight, and just like the duck, we often don't notice they are "a thing" because they are so much a part of us. I often use this highly sophisticated term, "a thing," in coaching sessions when we uncover an attribute, skill, or quality that we don't recognize as valuable and unique to us.

For example, I worked with a high school senior who told me he loved to organize closets. This strong masculine soccer player liked to organize his friends' closets while they were hanging out. "Isn't that interesting?!?" He definitely thought it was weird when he reluctantly told me about it.

He explained that he could not help himself. It made him crazy to be in the typical teenager disaster of a room that most of his friends occupied. This clue led us to his valuable skill and interest in organizing, which led to his choice of a college major in Logistics and Material Handling—an area that has an enormous organizational component.

Every piece of information is valuable, especially if it seems strange or out of the ordinary. Do you have "a thing?" You probably have many things. Let's go find them!

Mining for Gold

There are two approaches to uncovering your natural attributes.

One is to reflect on the qualitative information—the stories and examples from your past experiences.

- What seemed to come easily to you?
- What did you enjoy or feel about your experiences?
- How did you naturally do things?
- Where did you excel, or not?

We can also gain information from others' stories and experiences of us. This information is best gathered by asking other people about yourself—your spouse, friends, family, co-workers, teachers, etc. By asking questions and taking the time to reflect on the answers, you will start to make connections and gain insights. Great tools for this are personal journaling, storytelling, and talking it through with a trusted friend or your favorite career coach.

The second approach is quantitative information,

which is more scientific and possibly more objective.

Some readily available indicators are your grades, athletic records, and other academic test scores. These are important, but from my experience tell us very little about which direction, career or otherwise, is going to be fulfilling to you.

Today we have other, more useful quantitative tools that can get you there faster and more accurately. We have access to scientific assessments of all kinds in many different areas, like personality, strengths, and learning styles.

One caveat about assessments tools: make sure they are verified as being scientifically and statistically valid. A Facebook or magazine survey that tells you what actress or animal you are most like may be fun and give you some insight, but don't plan your life based on the results. This also goes for other online surveys or assessments that might seem credible at first glance.

The best way to find reliable tools is through consulting with a professional. Career coaches and other coaching professionals study, train, and pass testing for certifications in valuable tools that have been researched and validated for years or even decades. Seek these out.

I find the assessment tools I use in my coaching practice are eerily accurate and help people realize things they vaguely knew about themselves but could never put into words. For the first time, they recognize qualities they have that could be "a thing."

Your Natural Talents, Strengths, and Weaknesses

Let's start with a self-assessment of where you know you are naturally gifted.

- What are you good at?
- Are you naturally caring?
- Are you naturally inquisitive?
- Are you naturally analytical?
- What do you instinctively know how to do that no one taught or trained you? You just do it.

Often these are skills you are known for by your family, friends, and co-workers. People comment or compliment you on this as they witness you in action.

- What topics do people come to you for advice or help with?
- Which activities do you enjoy so much, time speeds by without you noticing?
- What abilities do you have that are effortless?
- What do you love to do or can't wait to do again?
- What do you do in your free time, that you

would never give up even if someone paid you to stop?

Conversely, where are your known weaknesses? These are as important to acknowledge as your gifts, except in this case, you want to avoid these things or to get support with dealing with them.

- What do you try to avoid at all cost?
- What have you attempted and know you will never master?
- What do you go to others for help with?
- What would you never try on your own?

Recommended Tool: *StrengthFinders 2.0* by Tom Rath.

StrengthFinders is a bestselling book created and distributed by the Gallup Research Organization. It explains in brief detail why defining and refining your natural strengths is essential and how to turn those strengths into skills.

StrengthFinders offers an online assessment that identifies your top five strengths out of the 34 their research has shown to be unique and useful. A few examples are Strategic, Relator, Empathy, and Learner. I really love what this assessment has to offer. My personal experience is if I don't get to use my top five strengths on a regular basis I am not very satisfied with my work.

Your Personality

Personality has to do with the unseen or intangible aspects of your character encompassing your natural behaviors and mannerisms, how you interact with people, and how you approach tasks. Personality is more than just being pleasant or funny. Are you positive or negative, outgoing or quiet, driven or laid back, kind or tough, logical or imaginative? How would you describe your personality?

Sometimes the people around you can more easily define your personality because they see you from the outside. They are impacted by your behaviors and can usually quickly describe your characteristics, both good and not so good. They can often see things about you that are hidden in your blind spot. So asking people you trust and respect to describe your personality is an exercise I often give my clients. Ask people who will be honest, caring, and willing to tell you the truth. This vulnerability can be a challenge, but the feedback is usually insightful and valuable.

Try asking 5-10 people to describe your personality.

Recommended Tool: There are many different personality assessment tools available: DiSC, Insights, etc. Each will have nuances that reveal various aspects of your personality and work style.

I primarily use the Myers-Briggs Type Indicator (MBTI) for career coaching as well as for leaders and work teams. Being the most widely utilized and researched assessment, there are many books and resources available based on the MBTI perspective of personalities. Just a reminder, please make sure practitioners of resources are credible. MBTI is one that can often be misrepresented in social media or online.

The MBTI is based on the work of renowned Swiss psychiatrist Carl Jung's theories about how people are naturally hardwired to experience the world. It addresses four primary areas:

1. Where do you get your energy: from people or alone?

2. How do you take in information: details or big picture?

3. How do you make decisions: logic or compassion?

4. How do you like your world to be organized: structured or unstructured?

When these four areas are combined, we get a distinct personality with consistent traits that can be aligned with career and life choices. It can also explain whether a particular work environment is conducive and nurturing or detrimental to each personality type. Although this tool is complex, it has a wealth of information to offer.

Incidentally, the MBTI is where our understanding of extrovert and introvert originated. Extroverts get their energy from people and the outside world. Introverts get their energy from time alone and personal reflection. Understanding this one aspect of yourself can be a game changer for your career as well as for purpose and self-acceptance.

Your Cognitive Abilities

How do you naturally think? And what is useful and unique about the way you think? When we consider cognitive ability, we usually think of school or being book smart: math, science, language arts, history, etc. Although this is useful information, it is a limited perspective. We may also think of IQ (Intelligence Quotient), which is another measurement of cognitive ability, but unless you are applying to the Massachusetts Institute of Technology (MIT) or Mensa, both known for educating geniuses, this is not much use to the everyday person.

I would rather you ask yourself, how are you smart? How does your brain work best? Howard Gardener, a neuropsychologist who introduced the theory of Multiple Intelligences in the 1980s, asked just this question. Gardener recognized and validated that there is more to intelligence than knowing school subjects. He broke up knowledge into 9 areas:

- Verbal/linguistic
- Logical/mathematical
- Visual/spatial

- Interpersonal/self-understanding
- Intrapersonal/people smart
- Naturalistic/understanding nature
- Bodily/kinesthetic
- Musical/rhythm and tone
- Existential/spiritual

You can easily see how identifying your native abilities could provide better insight into career direction and how you might achieve your purpose.

The MBTI also addresses a portion of cognitive ability, by asking how you take in information. "Detail" people are great with tangible or "real" things that can be counted or touched. Think mechanic or accountant. "Intuitive" people, on the other hand, are great with theory and abstract concepts. They are able to take bits of disconnected information and create a new solution or idea. Aren't all the capabilities and complexity of our brain fascinating?

There are still other aspects we have not addressed, like your memory, humor, focus, or speed of thought. All of these can point towards career and job satisfaction. Make this personal by asking yourself these questions:

- What do I want to think, talk about, or fix every day?

- What holds my attention and my heart?
- What makes me want to jump out of bed and get started every morning?

Your Physical Abilities

Your body is the wrapping or the package that holds Your Person and Your Soul. You can't change physical body characteristics like how tall you are, what color eyes you have, or whether or not you're going to lose your hair as you grow older. Physical abilities, on the other hand, are skills you can learn and develop mastery over. What physical abilities are natural to you?

What does "physical ability" even mean? When we hear that phrase, our mind goes directly to athletic prowess. Many people skip over the subject thinking it doesn't apply unless they are training to be a professional or Olympic athlete. Physical ability is so much more than excelling at a sport. Correctly assessed, it can be an indicator of how you will contribute from your magical blend of Soul, mind, and body.

Many career directions have physical attribute requirements that can be an asset to the job. Think of firefighters, pilots, tour guides, nurses, salespeople, broadcasters, florists, construction workers, musicians, doctors, and game testers.

Consider an actor or actress and how physical

attributes support their work. Not only is their appearance important, but also how they carry themselves and their body awareness - attributes that can help them adapt to fit a role. Other physical attributes to consider for actors are voice quality, charisma, and dancing ability.

Sometimes even gender plays a role. I was recently talking with the director of a trade school, who told me that women welders are currently needed in construction because of their smaller size and ability to get into tight spaces.

Consider these physical attributes: fine motor skills, strength, and rhythm. Are you a distance runner or a sprinter? Are you an early riser or a night owl?

Do people say you have charisma, sex appeal, or gracefulness? How are your vocal abilities, energy levels, and general health? Do you have exceptional balance, agility, or flexibility? What about your eyesight, eye-hand coordination, and reflexes?

All these are attributes suited to different career requirements.

Your Interests

What do you have an urge to learn more about? What do you crave to create, to do, or to experience? Think of subjects, activities, and causes you are naturally curious about or drawn to.

These urges are indicators of your interests because you instinctively know you will enjoy them or you are curious to find out if you actually do. Consider this: if I stood you in front of a huge magazine rack (I know—old school paper and ink, not a Kindle or tablet) with every topic available and left you for 20 minutes, what magazines would you pick up and look through?

Curiosity is a compelling starting point to finding your career and your purpose. Your curiosity just might be your Soul opening you up to the direction you need to go.

- What interest are you on your way to becoming an expert in?
- If you were asked to be on a radio show, what topic would you be interviewed about?
- What subject do you wish you were an expert in?
- Finish this sentence: "It would be out of this world to be known for ___."
- What did you love to do as a kid?
- What did you love as a kid that you gave up for adult responsibilities? I loved horses as a girl and recently started bringing them back into my life.
- What games did you like to play as a child? Make-believe, sports, war, teacher, post office, store?

Another way to look at interests, is to look at what movements or causes you would like to support or advance in the world?

- What are your biggest pet peeves?
- What would cause you to take action?
- What would you actually get off the couch to go do, no matter what time of day?
- What would you fight for, protest or picket?

These interests or causes that compel you to take action can tell you a ton about what is important to you.

Here are a few topics to consider (obviously the list could be infinite):

- Nature
- A specific sport
- Health
- Art
- Culture
- Children
- Social justice
- Travel

- Spirituality/religion
- Science
- A specific animal
- Hunting
- Entertainment
- History
- How things are made
- Mental health
- Outer space
- Organic gardening
- Oceans
- An era in time
- Decorating
- Baking
- Sewing
- Law
- Forensic science

- Video games

Recommended Tool: The *Strong Interest Inventory* is a tool I use to help discover the interests clients have and how those interests can connect directly to careers and purpose. This valuable tool gives the client a long laundry list of occupations to be ranked based on the best fit for their interests.

Your Experiences

There a few final things to consider, which may not be seen as attributes, but they are a part of Your Person. Your experiences up to this point in your life are also attributes and assets.

Here are a few examples:

- Eldest child
- Divorced
- Well-traveled
- Grew up on a farm
- College dropout
- Parent
- Poetry contest winner
- City kid
- Accident survivor

- Appeared on television
- Disabled
- Grew up sheltered

These or similar experiences are as unique as you are. Even if you and your siblings had the same outward experiences, you each internalized them differently, preparing you for your unique destinations.

Your past experiences, whether you see them as positive or negative, planned or accidental, life-affirming or disastrous, are uniquely yours. They serendipitously give you the strength, knowledge, confidence, courage, insight or even desperation to prepare you for your purpose.

These life lessons might serve as stepping stones leading to your purpose, or they might be the catalyst that abruptly turned you toward your destiny. Take stock of them, acknowledge the lessons, then decide to get out of bed and keep on going.

- What are some of the toughest challenges you have experienced?
- What did you learn about life or living from those experiences?
- How have those experiences prepared you for new experiences?

New Experiences

I am a huge advocate of trying new things. New experiences are critical because you don't truly know if you have an affinity for something until you try it firsthand! You may have a preconceived notion that is entirely wrong. It's like ice cream - if you have only eaten vanilla, how do you know it's your favorite? How do you know Chunky Monkey® or New York Super Fudge Chunk® isn't your favorite? In fact, you should try all the flavors, just to be sure.

It's human nature for other people to try and guide us based on their own experiences, especially our families. Although intended to be helpful, this can often block us from trying new things and developing our personal preferences. Sure, listen to others, take their advice, and then go experience it for yourself. Just go out and try things. Do your research with your own body and check in with your body compass along the way.

One of my pet peeves is when people write off new experiences saying, "I can't do that, I don't know how." Duh! Of course, you don't know how, you have never tried it. That is why it is new! What these people are actually saying is "I am afraid to try… what if I look stupid?"

If you expect to be great at everything on the first try, you are going to live a very limited life. Were you an accomplished driver the first time you got behind the wheel? Of course not! It took practice before you got comfortable and good at it. Confidence comes with action. Now, being a good driver doesn't necessarily mean you want to zip around a race track at 150 mph or become a long-haul trucker, but how will you ever know if you don't try driving in the first place?

Optimal Experiences

The point to all this taking stock of your natural attributes (Your Person) is to find your optimal experience(s). Optimal experiences are the ideal possibilities you are nervously elated to try because all the pieces of Your Person and Your Soul seem to click together.

- What would be the ideal experiences and direction for you?

- Where do all the pieces come together for you?

- What seems to be hot, even red hot, to your body compass?

- What feels like falling in love?

- What makes your Soul quake?

- What compels you to take action?

- What do you want so much that you are willing to do the hard stuff to get there? (I know we have the right major when my student clients can answer this question with confidence.)

- What would you do if you knew you would be, without a doubt, wildly successful, and your family and friends were 100% supportive?

Success and meaning will come to you when you follow these optimal experiences like breadcrumbs to your unique purpose-driven destination. When you align your Soul and Person to a life full of optimal experiences, life keeps getting better and better. In this environment the possibilities are endless.

You may respond with, "Yeah, but I have responsibilities." Or, "Yeah, but there are no guarantees." Or perhaps, "Yeah, but what if I screw it up and fail?"

In the next section, we will address why we struggle to give ourselves permission to take full action on these optimal experiences.

Resource: You can find the link to download a workbook containing these questions at the end of the book.

A Story to Bring It Together for You

My brother, Jason, is one of the leaders in the Los Angeles County School System. It is interesting how a Catholic schoolboy from Indiana got from there to where he is now. When he was young, he was tall for his age. In first grade, the school had to bring a fourth grade-sized desk in for him so he could sit comfortably.

He was a likable kid, and a bit hard-headed. His size and his tendency to be a rascal got him in trouble more often than our parents liked.

In his 8th-grade year, Jason got into some real trouble. He had turned into a bit of a hoodlum. Through the discipline that sports offered and with the help of our parents, he turned himself around. It was hard work and took a relentless commitment from him and my parents.

By the time he was a senior in high school, his football team had won the state championships, and he decided he wanted to play college football. Along the way, he began to focus on education and coaching. When he graduated from college, he went to work at Pasadena High School in Los Angeles - a very rough school. He was really good at his job, and there was something about his experience of growing up a little wild and having been caught up in the hoodlum lifestyle that helped him see what kids needed and were thinking. He could talk to them and communicate on a level they understood.

Ten years later, he became a dean for a charter school system that specialized in work with "last chance" students in South, Central, and East L.A. Jason worked with former gang leaders who were helping kids stay on the straight and narrow. Now he works for L.A. County, with students who are incarcerated and experiencing challenges on many different levels.

Jason is smart, charismatic, street savvy, and caring. He is also able to disconnect enough to avoid getting sucked into the kids' emotional drama or to let circumstances in the community wear him down. He's brave. He's kind of a little crazy and ideally suited for this road he's taken. This is an excellent example of how a person's natural abilities, skills, past experience, and professional interests all came together to make him excel at his job and serve in the way that he does.

Did he plan every step along the way? No, but he followed one hot spot after another, saying "This is a good choice for me. This looks like a good fit. This seems like an exciting challenge."

He found his way by following his "optimal experiences." Working with these troubled youngsters was intriguing to him. He intentionally chose to work with them. He would literally go to the public school principals and say, "Give me your worst kids," and move them to a place where they could get a lot more help and support.

When you follow the things you find intriguing, things that have meaning to you, you are on the right track. Jason is doing phenomenal things, using his talents and skills to support and change schools. His experience of getting off course as a youth himself offered him a perspective that led him to become an expert in his field.

By using his personality and his optimal experiences,

Jason continues to live his Soul's goal. One thing to note, Jason's path didn't necessarily happen entirely by design or by following what might be considered a formula for success. He just did whatever the hell he wanted to, and he didn't care what anybody else thought, even his wife. Understandably, you can see her concern for his safety.

Jason's ability to give himself permission, quiet his fears, and follow his optimal experiences has been the essential key to his success. As his older sister, it has been incredible to watch his transformation from my punk, pain-in-the-ass brother to someone I admire for the man he has become.

PART 3: Your SOCIAL SELF

The third and final part of your Personal Trilogy is called your Social Self. Your Social Self has internalized all the messages from your environment: family, friends, school, religion, media, and society. These messages have been accumulated during your life so far, and your Social Self dictates these rules and standards you have come to live by, both consciously and subconsciously.

I confess, the Social Self has gotten a pretty bad rap. In this book, I have made the Social Self out to be the "bad guy" or villain in your life. Maybe that is not true for you. Maybe the standards you have set for yourself have gotten you very far, maybe much further than anyone ever in your family, maybe further in success, quality of life, and happiness. That is fantastic! Keep it up!

If that's the case, why are you here? Go live all that is possible for you! Just do it! Go now, put down this book and take action!

Wait… why are you still reading this? Just go live life to the fullest! You got this!

It is not so easy to "Just do it!" is it? Sorry Nike, "Just do it," just doesn't work for most of us.

Why? Because each of us has different Social Self messages we have adopted and allowed to rule our lives. Your Social Self itself is not a negative force—it wants to keep you safe. But your Social Self may not be living by the rules that allow your Soul to find its way to best love and serve the world. Its rules may not match up with what is possible or meant for you. If this is you, you are going to feel the conflict.

For example, maybe your Social Self makes you more cautious rather than going for the "Just do it" mentality. The concept of *really just doing anything* is probably going to seem a bit irresponsible and maybe even insane. But you need to take some calculated risks to discover and create the life you want. You need to learn to manage your Social Self so you can live the life you desire.

For some of us, the Social Self lessons we have internalized empower our lives. There are countless people on this road. If your Social Self is your personal cheerleader, great! If you are having success and your standards of excellence are consistent and nurturing, it is because your Social Self adopted the behaviors that got you there. If you are there, wonderful!

If you aren't there yet, I want you to know that it is possible. I have yet to meet anyone who does not bump up against thoughts of self-doubt and deep-seated beliefs that cause hesitation or inaction at times. That includes my brother, who I discussed in the last chapter, as well as all of my clients.

The Social Self has layers like an onion, and as you peel back a layer of thoughts and beliefs, there is often another layer waiting to be questioned and considered as either useful or needing to be transformed into something that will help rather than restrict you.

The Social Self is complicated at best. As we prepare to dive deeper into Social Self, start by asking yourself these core questions.

- Is your Social Self based in fear or compassion?
- Does it have a limited or fixed mindset? Or is it based on a loving "anything is possible" growth mindset?
- Do you think you are always right? Or are you willing to examine your thinking and see where it may not be working?
- Are you willing to change the way you think to get different or better results?

When you are willing to study your thinking, release those beliefs that hold you back, and adopt new and improved beliefs, I am not exaggerating when I say this is where the magic or even miracles start to happen.

When we have beliefs that make our natural selves feel unworthy or that prevent us from living or seeing the purpose that compels us, our Soul is trapped and suffocated. When we adjust our Social Self to align with our Soul and not the other way around, things radically change for the better.

If I believed because I was an outsider to that little town in Ohio and that I had no business speaking up, or if I let myself believe my ideas were silly, the Komminsk Legacy Park would have never been built. Believe me, my Social Self tried to get me to accept those thoughts, but I chose not to listen and instead I embraced the anything-is-possible mindset, which made all the difference in turning that park from a dream into reality.

Anatomy of Your Social Self

Our brains at their most primal are programmed to keep us safe and alive. We have basic needs that are critical to survival. Things like air, water, food, shelter, and human connection. It is our brain's job to first and foremost assure these resources are available so that we can survive and function. This means our natural built-in reflexes, learning, and problem-solving skills are continuously on the lookout for potential threats to these needs.

As young children, we rapidly learn all kinds of information from observing, listening, and mimicking those around us. This assures our survival and enables us to grow and thrive. From the time we are infants we are literally absorbing every action, word, and emotional reaction - storing their messages away in our database-like brain. Everything we store can then be accessed for future use. This intentional or unintentional learning, blended with our natural personality, impacts how we see the world and adds to how our Social Self views the world.

This learning imprints on us programming we carry with us, and it becomes part of our survival reflexes—teaching us what is perceived to be right or wrong, good or bad, and safe or unsafe behavior.

This learning is also influenced by the frequency we receive specific messages, and the emotional impact situations and people have on us. The impact is easy to see in young children when they correct someone else with the exact language they hear from their caregivers. "We don't say, 'Shut Up,' Daddy. That is not nice!" Kids hear the word "no" so often before they are 3, it's no wonder their favorite word back to grownups is "No!"

Some messages are beneficial, like "Look both ways before you cross the street." This teaches us an outstanding survival skill. But "The dark is scary," is not a very useful message when you are trying to get your kids to bed every night. It's also not helpful later when they need to walk down the street to a night class on their college campus, or when they are 78 and need to get up to go the bathroom three times a night in their dark house. Beliefs can stay with us for our entire lives.

Learning is also affected by the primal need for acceptance. We're constantly looking for acceptance, first from our families, but also as we get older from our peers, teachers, coworkers, and society. This innate need is built into our psyche from our pre-historic ancestors who knew there was safety in numbers, that to be shunned often meant starvation and death.

Research shows over and over that humans crave connection with other humans for healthy development, both intellectually and emotionally. So knowing and doing what is acceptable and keeps you connected is essential, but doing what pleases others or living your life by what is acceptable to society does not always equate to being who you truly are or living your extraordinary life.

To understand this dynamic, all I need to say is three words, "junior high girls." Junior high girls are the classic example of needing to be accepted by pleasing others—even to the point of hurting others' feelings and themselves in their attempts to be accepted. During the junior high years many girls leave sports or activities they love because they are not considered "cool" anymore. They lose their confidence, and their body images change because they are comparing themselves to others and worrying that they don't measure up.

These wounds get deeper when even as grown women we don't always curb our need for acceptance and the urge to please others. Very often in my workshops, women share that they don't know what they want or prefer in their careers and lives because they have been attempting to please others for so long. They have ignored their own needs and wants for so long they don't know their own preferences.

We think giving away this power was a 1950's problem, but it is still happening today. Acceptance is important in moderation, but letting it drive your life can be destructive.

Don't get me wrong; I don't think that we as humans are trying to pull each other away from our purpose. We genuinely are trying to help each other—well maybe not the girls in junior high—but most everyone else, and especially our parents, want the best for us. Of course parents love their children and want to support their success in life. Parents are first and foremost trying to keep their children safe, and they are doing the best they can. But remember they are working from their own Social Self perspective and biases and aren't always aware what their children need to connect with their Soul's goal.

For example, a few years ago I took 12 students

from our rural area on a tour of an art and design college in a bigger city. These high school juniors were talented in many different art forms, but they were continuously getting the message that you can't be an artist and make any money. Their parents and communities were giving them the 'starving artist' message over and over again.

So I took them on tour to see what different types of art are taught and what designers actually do. Every pair of shoes, every purse, every piece of clothing, every book cover, every car, every appliance, and every cell phone—all are designed for form and function by industrial, fashion, and graphic designers. All these products are manufactured in our region and have a designer's hand in creating or selling them. There are many jobs in these fields. The parents simply did not know about the many different ways you can make money as an artist.

When these kids continually get the message that artists don't make money from the people they trust, they start to believe it. This squelches the possibility that they could grow up to be an artist and that being an artist can be a valuable and productive career. Yes, there's a practical side to consider. But when you repress the idea that becoming an artist may be your Soul's goal, you might end up going through life doing something mundane and meaningless, rather than studying art and design, where your talents lie, and your Soul can soar.

How do parents come to pass on the starving artist message? It is a message they received from the society they live in, and until they have new evidence or a fresh perspective, that belief is not going to change. It will only be strengthened and perpetuated. This is why seeking to reevaluate rules you live by is so essential.

Habits of Thinking

As we take in information as youngsters, the brain naturally attempts to make sense of all of it. In this process, we begin internalizing the lessons and making them our own. As we put together our personal perspective of the world, like a stained-glass window, it gives us a unique view of how we see the world. Every new experience, situation, and message gets filtered through our window and added to our view or is dismissed and thrown away because it does not match what we have come to know and believe.

So we start repeating the same line of thinking, and that thought becomes a habit. A habit in the brain is an electric pulse being sent down the same neuro-pathway over and over until it is an automatic reflex. Think about when you learned to drive a car. At first, it took a lot of thinking and attention to make sure you did everything right. Then after a few weeks, it became easier for you. Now driving is second nature and you don't think about the steps it takes to drive at all. They just happen.

The same thing happens with our Social Self. When

we first learn something, we must work hard to make the pulses go down a new path in our brain. Then as we practice, the new pathways get stronger and smoother. The newly learned action takes less effort, and we get faster and better at what we're doing. After lots of practice and repetition, the skill or action happens without much effort at all.

Your Social Self is on autopilot. This ease is part of the brain's survival plan, causing you to act on ingrained beliefs and rules, without pausing to consider whether they help or hinder your progress. Here are a few habits of thinking that come from the Social Self.

Social Self based Fear

With our brain's priority to keep us safe and secure, it is naturally on the lookout for threats to our survival or well being. This habit of thinking can be reinforced or calmed by our experiences, upbringing, and our natural personality.

Fear is a natural response meant to give you a quick burst of energy for your protection. When we experience or imagine threats, fear is the typical emotional response.

When the brain senses fear it goes into fight, flight, please, or freeze mode. Your brain is protecting you. The problem is when you are protecting yourself, you are not connecting to your Soul or your body. Your brain is focusing on the threat, not on connecting to your inner wisdom.

Fear limits your creativity and ability to be loving and rational. Think about the last time you got angry. If you reflect on the situation, I bet you felt threatened. Some fear was triggered, and you went into fight or flight mode. I also bet you said things you regret, possibly in an irrational or otherwise not constructive manner. Or perhaps you went into please or freeze mode, then spent the next two days rehashing your response or rehearsing a better one in your head. This is destructive, not to mention a waste of your time and energy.

Feeling fear is good when there is a real danger. By all means, run! Or if there's a rattlesnake in your sleeping bag, back away slowly!

But is the threat real or imaged? Ironically, in modern Western society research shows only 8% percent of our common fears are valid. This means all the things we routinely worry about are statistically never going happen. You will have food and shelter and people who love you. You will never be a bag lady living under the bridge down by the river with a guy named Gus!

Your fears, more often than not, are not realistic, even if you believe they are. They are "phantom" fears straight out of your imagination. You may have heard this popular acronym for fear: False Evidence Appearing Real.

Here is why that happens. No matter what, your brain will never stop protecting you. It will always stay on the lookout for threats, so much so that it may invent threats to protect you from. Now, this is fine if we can playfully watch a zombie horror movie. It's why we enjoy fictional scary things like haunted houses, survival television, and video games. These give our brains something to "protect" us from. But this primal reflex can also allow fear to grow unchecked, resulting in unnecessary worry and anxiety.

This is why I dislike the traditional news sources, which focus on all the negative "news-worthy" stories. For every bad thing that gets reported, there are thousands of good things happening that go unnoticed. And unlike the scary fictional stories, these things are really happening.

When we put our attention on negative news instead of positive news, we make matters worse. We go into fear mode and start to hyperfocus, which raises our fight and flight reflex. Then we become angry and stressed and react negatively towards others, or we limit our lives as a by-product of fear. I stopped watching the news many years ago, knowing the important information will get to me. My life is much happier and more peaceful because of it.

So think about the one thing you worry about most often. What are you afraid of? What stops you from living the life you want? Maybe you are afraid of what other people will think. Maybe you are afraid of making a mistake or of failure. Maybe you want to swim the English Channel but are afraid of sharks, cold water, or wearing a Speedo. Maybe you are afraid to write a book that is burning to get out.

Does your Social Self have a habit of thinking bad things will happen? Do these thoughts paralyze you or make you want to take action? What habits of fearful thinking do you have? Do you believe that life is generally safe and good or it is unsafe and dangerous? These significant nuances of thinking can be your saboteur or your motivation to move forward. You get to decide when you start to realize you have a choice.

Sabotage by Self-Talk

Another habit that can sabotage us is self-talk. Self-talk is the conversation that runs endlessly in your head—measuring and judging your behavior. It is the voice of your Social Self repeating all those internalized life lessons that you apply to critique yourself, to measure if the way you are living is good and safe.

This internal dialogue can be your biggest critic, telling you what you are doing is wrong. Fear and negativity can become a strong influence if you don't keep the negativity in check. Your Social Self can also be your cheerleader giving you pep talks along the way, depending on whether you have adopted a fearful or a loving perspective.

You can actually have both voices speaking at the same time. You may remember the old television scenarios were an angel sits on one shoulder, and the devil sits on the other. But instead of good or bad advice, the Social Self is spewing negative or positive thoughts. When both voices are making their case, it can be confusing and is often why people get stuck. They simply don't know which way to go.

You will hear coaches, like me, refer to your "gremlins"—those negative, demeaning voices that we all hear in our heads. Gremlins are imaginary characters from a 1980s movie called, shockingly, Gremlins. In the movie these fuzzy, cute, sweet creatures would become terribly destructive monsters when left alone to eat and go crazy after midnight. You can have a warm, friendly relationship with your gremlins—your Social Self and judge—or you can let them run rampant, spreading their negativity and being destructive in your life.

This is critical information because some negative self-talk can stall us and keep us off track, or drive us to make detrimental decisions. I believe negative self-talk and fear are where pain and evil originate. If a young man's gremlins constantly say, "You are so stupid, you idiot!" and he believes it, he is not going to try very hard in school, because he sees no point. He may even drop out. Then he becomes desperate to make a living. He feels so bad he tries drugs to escape, and his life just keeps spiraling out of control. Self-talk is powerful, and we have the power to change it, but first, we must realize that we are doing it.

Say out loud to yourself right now. "I am awesome and extraordinary, and I can create everything I desire in my life!"

Now wait. What is the thought you had right after saying that? It usually starts with "Yeah but," or "Except I can't," or "If only I weren't." Maybe you laugh at how outlandish or impossible "awesome and extraordinary" sounds.

Those responses are your gremlin's favorite crappy tunes that they love to spew at you under the guise of keeping you safe from change or growth. Write them down. Most of the time we don't even know we are saying them because we are on autopilot. This self-talk is a deeply ingrained habit. Every time we repeat these things to ourselves we are reinforcing them, and we continue to believe they are true.

Here are some of the things I have heard over the years from friends and clients.

- "You are so stupid."
- "You look like an idiot."
- "You will never be good/pretty/smart enough."
- "No one really cares."
- "You don't know what you're doing."

My number one gremlin crappy song is "You're a

mess!" It's like an angry hard rock song that has a catchy hook I can't get out of my head. This is my Social Self telling me, "Yes, you could do anything you want, if only you weren't such a mess, so disorganized, and such a procrastinator! So why would you even try!" This is so self-defeating.

You have the power to listen, to reflect, and to choose your self-talk. It is life changing when you realize this. You can pause, get off autopilot and think:

- Is this my true belief?
- Do I want to perpetuate this thinking?
- How does this thinking impact my behavior and my life?
- Can I start to select a different message that would be more beneficial?
- What message could I tell myself instead—something that is believable and helps me move forward?

Here are my questions and answers to my gremlin crappy thought:

How do I feel when I believe this thought, "I am a mess"?
I feel awful, embarrassed and incapable!

How do I react or behave?

I am debilitated. I don't want to do a thing. I want to hide.

So, does it help me to say this to myself or to believe it?
No!

Is this thought true? Can I think of times when it is not true?
Well no—it isn't true because I have a family, household, and business that I run. I accomplish all kinds of things that prove I'm not a mess. I may have a little chaos and disorganization in my life, but clearly, I am also on top of it.

What is another thought or statement that is truer than "I'm a mess" that would serve me better?
I am getting better. As I step into new challenges, I am learning and getting better every time. (Notice this is not a radically different thought like "I am perfect. Everything I do is perfect." Our brain does not easily believe the radical opposite of a gremlin thought. What's important is that the statement is truer than the original statement and gives you a degree of relief.)

How do you feel when you believe this truer statement?
I feel like I can breathe and continue to get better. It motivates me to keep trying.

The Work

Much of this technique is referred to as "The Work" which originated with author Byron Katie. To dive deeper into the power of changing limiting thoughts, read more from her or watch the compelling videos on her website.

I have one client who simply switched her self-talk from "You can't do this," to a loving supportive "You got this, baby girl!" It made a huge difference for her. Notice the importance of self-compassion in these new truer statements. The goal is not to make yourself feel worse about your self-talk, but to adjust it to empower you.

Interestingly, at times what you hear in your head is the voice and words your parents, caregivers or significant people spoke to you.

- "Mary, you are too outspoken. No one wants to hear your jabbering."
- "You are getting too big for your britches, don't be a show-off."
- "Just be a good girl and do what you are told."
- "You are such a mean person. Don't say things that may upset others."

It is not unusual as my clients start recognizing the source of their self-talk to need to come to terms with the pain they endured growing up. Most often this process of assessment helps people heal and become responsible for their own lives and self-talk rather than relying on the past as their only source of self-worth.

When I was a kid, my mom used this one in jest as she brushed out my long, tangled hair, "You must suffer to be beautiful." Nice, right? (Insert my eye roll here.) She heard it from the nuns in the orphanage where she grew up. Even in jest, it stuck with me.

Ironically when I think about it, the lesson I internalized was that beauty was bad. Beauty equaled suffering. I didn't want to suffer, therefore I didn't want to be beautiful. I felt sorry for and had disdain for girls who were attractive. As you can imagine, this lesson didn't help me in junior high. Then it occurred to me in high school that everyone, including me, could be beautiful and my self-talk changed.

Resource: You can find the link to download a workbook containing these questions at the end of the book.

Meaning Making and Social Self Talk

Imagine that your boss comes to work, goes into her office, and closes the door without saying a word. What meaning do you give her actions? Is there something wrong? Is she angry? Is she angry with you? Did your report yesterday not meet her expectations? Maybe she has realized you're not very good at your job. Maybe you should start looking for a new one. Why did you buy that new car? Will you be fired today or tomorrow?

Your Social Self wails, "But I don't want to move back in with my parents!"

Just then your boss emerges from her office with a warm, "Good morning. I had a great idea and I just had to get it down before I lost the inspiration."

This is an example of meaning-making, the third habit of thinking connected to our Social Self. Meaning-making is giving meaning to a situation in a way that is not based on facts but on assumptions from our past experiences or the Social Self messages we have learned. Meaning-making can impact our feelings, our reactions, our behaviors, and consequently our outcomes in positive or negative ways.

As we gather our Social Self messages growing up and going through life, we start to make sense of all this information. We internalize and filter our perspective of the world. We create that stained-glass window we see the world through. When meaning-making goes unchecked, we think our meaning is the only one there is, the correct one, so we only gather information that supports and strengthens that belief.

When we start to realize not all situations or people are the same we can begin to reserve our judgment and be open to new understanding and different outcomes.

Much like the example I offered in the previous section about internalizing beauty as a bad thing; it was not only my mom's message as a young girl that brought me to that conclusion. There were many other messages that influenced the same perspective, including being excluded by the girls in my class for being awkward in middle school, and cousins teasing me when I tried to be fashionable. Give me a break! It was the late 70's and 80's.

The habit of meaning-making becomes a struggle when we apply our personal meaning to every situation we encounter. Although I rationally know it is misguided, I am still a little suspect of beautiful people when I first meet them. If I was unaware of this habit, I could easily sabotage new friendships and possibly my business. So instead I recognize this reaction in myself and choose a different, more productive perspective or meaning based on love and kindness.

Because I have been able to do this, I now have many friends who are beautiful inside and out. In fact, I have had the opportunity to coach several junior beauty pageant contestants. What I have learned is that everyone, even those considered beautiful, questions their worthiness and needs encouragement.

All of us are constantly making meaning—you too. Something happens, and you have a thought about it, you give it meaning. Your brain (specifically the hypothalamus) is categorizing it.

When information arrives, in a fraction of a second

your brain has two questions: Is this dangerous? And where does this fit in our experience? The new event gets compared to your past events and stored in your memory, kind of like when you save a file to a computer. The meaning comes from past experiences or data collected previously.

Because this process is on autopilot, your Social Self is in control, ensuring that biases, emotional triggers, and fears will be your first reaction if you feel even mildly threatened. Or if your brain files the event in the good, interesting, or loving file your reaction will follow that line of thinking. These are usually subconscious reactions unless we bring them into our consciousness by noticing and paying attention to the thought or the emotion. Until we have this awareness, we can't begin to manage our thinking differently.

The goal of understanding your meaning-making habits is to be aware of what they are and to adjust the ones that don't serve your Soul's goal to turn them into meanings that can help you get along better in life. You can override the thoughts that don't serve you and select better ones that align with your purpose.

I find this knowledge especially valuable with big-picture thinking. Here are three examples of consciously deciding to make more useful meanings that have changed my life.

Original thought: My husband's and my kid's job is to make me happy.

New thought: It is 100% up to me to choose thoughts and actions that will make myself happy.

Original thought: Life and making money is hard.
New thought: Life and making money can come with ease when I am playful, follow my heart, realize my value, do great work, and welcome God/Universe to co-create with me.

Original thought: Because there are a limited number of people who need my services, I need to fight for clients and be a true competitor.
New thought: There are plenty of people who need support and help. My job is to let them know I am here and how I can help. They will decide if I have what they need.

What meanings are you habitually making that pull you off track or make life harder?

The key to becoming aware is to notice judgments you may be making, areas that bring you stress, or things that trigger a strong emotional reaction. Notice the events that cause those reactions.

Ask yourself, "Why does this bother me?"

Then ask yourself, "Why is (the answer) so important to me?"

Then continue by asking yourself, "Why is that answer important?"

Keep asking yourself these questions until you get

to the core of the issue and what triggers it.

When you have the core of this belief identified, like "My husband should make me happy," turn the statement around or replace words until you get to a statement that resonates with you as truer or gives you a little Soul quake.

"I should make my husband happy," is an easy turnaround, but when I tried "I should make myself happy," I felt the truth of it and knew I had the right answer.

Teach your Social Self how to question thoughts, and practice thinking and saying better ones until this becomes your new habit of thinking.

Compassionate Self Image

The final habit of thinking is your self image. It is literally, you guessed it, the image you have of yourself. In your mind when you picture yourself, how do you see yourself?

Now, this is different than Your Person because Your Person is your natural attributes, gifts, and weakness in physical form. Self image is how your Social Self sees or perceives you. It is about imagination—how you imagine yourself to be. An example is when someone believes they are fat or ugly and clearly they are not. It does not matter what is true. It is what they believe about themselves, and this drives how they treat themselves.

Your self image comes from many different

influences in your life experiences and dictates how you present yourself to the world. The image we have of ourselves is powerful and can empower and motivate us for good, or it can be detrimental and limit us.

Think about the simple implication of being referred to as a girl versus a woman, or a boy versus a man. What image do you have of yourself when you embody or imagine yourself as either one of those? Try a wife or a mother, a husband or a father. How about a grandparent? Now, try a leader. Or a troublemaker. What about a saint? A brain? A whore? A clown?

It is compelling to consider the image that comes up when you imagine yourself as these different labels. If you actually started to believe any one of these, think about how differently you would feel about yourself. How differently would you behave? Would you have different expectations of yourself? How would your relationships change? What ultimately would your outcomes in life be? Your imagination is powerful—especially when you apply it to yourself.

So what is your image of yourself? For most of us, it is complicated because of the different roles we play throughout our lives, day to day and year to year. But at the core, like a character in a novel, what is the story you tell about yourself? What is your self image?

The more closely your self image aligns with pride and self-compassion with Your Person and Your Soul, the healthier you are, and the more comfortable you are in your skin. You are happy when you are authentic—true to who you are. When the three are not aligned, your Social Self has hijacked your self image. And your habits of thinking are rooted in fear.

For example, when you continually fulfill others' expectations, you are trying to squeeze yourself into an inauthentic label, or you may be shaming or not valuing parts of your true self. By not allowing the complexity of who you are to be a welcomed part of your self image, you limit and judge and belittle yourself instead of looking at your attributes as potentially valuable.

This hit home for me when I took the StrengthsFinder Assessment. One of my top five strengths is "WOO" which stands for Winning Others Over. When I first read this, I was upset. I equated that idea to acting like a used car salesman, unethically talking people into buying things they don't need and worse, swindling them. When I imagined myself as that it made me feel icky. I did not want to be that!

As I soaked in this idea that I had this strength of "WOO," and I read more about its true meaning, I realized it was an incredibly valuable strength. It is only icky to me when used for self-serving or unethical purposes. I found I used it mostly when I was speaking on a motivational topic to uplift people or when I was teaching a new idea that could help people change their lives. When I embraced this skill and started to hone it, I became increasingly effective when coaching and convincing stubborn executives or physicians to try new thinking and behaviors for better results with their staff and customers.

Winning others over is a part of who I am and when I own it and embody it, WOO is a compelling and invaluable part of me.

Social Self Labels

We have a habit of giving ourselves labels and living up to the stereotypes associated with those labels. Most labels are self-imposed or dictated by what we learn from society. But labels can also come from messages we got directly from others in our family or social circles. Things like "she is the smart one" or "he is the black sheep."

Other labels come from society: a musician, a poor person, an intellectual, an artist, a country boy, a rebel, a health nut, a tree hugger, a boss, an engineer, and an entrepreneur are just a few out of hundreds of examples. If I say any one of these, you have a preconceived image of what these people are, what they do, and how they "should" act or behave. The problem is that labels are one dimensional, and humans are much more complex than a label suggests. Take it from a belly dancing, free spirited, professional, oldest child, animal lover, consultant, mother, college educated, recovering band nerd, wife, world traveler, dyslexic, conservative liberal, life and career coach, like me.

The power of labels is the theme of one of my favorite movies, The Breakfast Club. In this movie, the characters, all high school students, portray stereotypes of the jock, the hoodlum, the nerd, the beauty queen, and the weirdo. They are all stuck together in detention one Saturday. The plot uncovers the angst of being labeled and labeling yourself. Some of the many morals of the movie are: embrace who you are, life can be tough no matter who you are, and you are not stuck in a stereotype.

What are some of the different ways you label yourself?

- Are they healthy labels?
- How are they driven by your Social Self?
- How are you allowing those labels to empower you or stifle you?

A few labels that are especially charged for people are victim, dumb, addict, unworthy, unlovable, hopeless, useless, or failure. If you see yourself as any of these labels, please get some support through counseling or coaching. These labels have ruined lives since the beginning of time. No matter what you believe about yourself, you can overcome these thoughts and make your life extraordinary. There are people like me waiting to help you: people who have tackled and mastered these mountains, people whose Soul's Goal is to climb up with you.

If you are determined to climb through this darkness alone, here is a place to start.

Mistakes and Forgiveness

If you have been letting your Social Self run the show most of your life, you have had problems. Guaranteed. After a lifetime of living with fear, which always generates a lack, attack, fight, or flight response, you have made some mistakes. Probably even some big ones. You probably hurt some people, and most likely you are one of those people you have hurt—maybe unknowingly, maybe unintentionally, maybe even purposely. You know what I'm talking about.

Your fear and the associated negative response becomes a habitual way of thinking, which you equate to your self image. Maybe you think you can't live any differently. Where do you think thoughts like the following will lead you?

> "I am a bad person because I stole that candy at 10 and that car at 15 and now I am cheating on my wife and taxes. This is who I am, and I can't change."

This thought pattern defines you by your mistakes. Once you believe this is who you are, the downward spiral begins, deeper and deeper until you think there is no way out.

You are not your mistakes.

The truth is that you are not that person at your core. You have just lost your way. You bought into the fear and didn't believe or know how you could be different. Most likely, love in some form was missing from your life or not touching your heart. Of course, your gremlins are in control, like guards on the prison walls preventing love from getting in.

You probably missed or ignored the direct messages from your body compass: indicators called shame and guilt, those super yucky feelings in the pit of your stomach. These are messages from your Soul saying, "Warning! Warning! This is not who you really are, you can go another way." Maybe you have lived with these feelings since you were an infant and you didn't know you could feel differently. So when things went wrong, you added those negative results to your pile of evidence that confirmed what you already believed about yourself.

Believing you are a bad person and not worthy of a good life makes having an extraordinary life seem impossible, much less even considering that your Soul has some grand goal! But you are worthy, and you have a mission. Overcoming the devastating belief that your mistakes define you may be the first step towards finding that mission.

Think about it: the most inspiring stories are the ones where someone overcame a real obstacle, the big challenge of their life. They came back from the depths of despair and darkness. Who are you to think this can't happen to you too!?!

Who are you to back down from the challenge that has been laid at your feet? Facing those fears head-on is the answer to believing you are worthy by fighting the gremlins to take back your life.

Ironically the best way to fight a gremlin is to give it compassion and forgiveness, to give yourself compassion and forgiveness. But self-forgiveness doesn't come easily. We are often in denial about the amount of pain we were in that lead to causing someone else's pain. It takes honesty and courage to look back on something so raw. It is not an easy thing to do. Your ability to get "real" with yourself about your past is an essential part of the way to real forgiveness.

So we examine our own pain, and how it got there, and how that caused the mistakes we have made. By having self-compassion and empathy for how we reacted to our own Social Self messages, we can start to understand how we went down this road. This doesn't mean we are justifying our mistakes, but rather that we are being honest and aware so we don't make the same mistakes again.

Next, we need to get real about the depth of the pain we have caused others. Without this empathy and sorrow for those we hurt, our forgiveness is shallow. Owning our mistakes, apologizing, and working to do better are essential parts of the path to forgiveness, finding our true self, and moving towards our Soul.

We cannot change our past, but by coming to terms with it, by healing ourselves, and becoming a force for good in the world, we defeat those gremlins and start believing in our true value.

Self Image Reinvention

One of the challenges of adopting a label or a role is holding on to it too tightly. Many people will hold their initial beliefs about themselves their entire lives and get stuck there. This is what happened with Robert. If you recall Robert was my client who wanted to play college baseball, and when he didn't get that dream, he ended up stuck and depressed. He did not know who to be next, so he opted for partying until he found a new role as a finance student, and now as a professional.

Marie could not see herself as a retail manager or college graduate or survivor, but she got there.

Louise had to reinvent herself into a powerful, talented single woman.

My brother, Jason, had to let go of being a troublemaker to become an athlete and later a teacher, then a dean, now a school district leader.

We have to let go of who we think we are to see who we can become. The transition can be much smoother when we start by dreaming of a new version of ourselves. Then we can begin to let go of the old self image and adopt the new persona or image of ourselves.

This ability to keep reinventing ourselves is the skill that will assure our success for the many transitions we all face in life. Take these organic transitions: a daughter/son to wife/husband to mother/father to grandmother/grandfather. If you only think of yourself as a son or daughter, when you become a spouse or a parent, life is going to be a struggle. Your image of yourself must evolve so you can step into the necessary mindset, behaviors, and responsibilities of a new role in life. If you don't evolve, your success will be limited at best.

We all have a self image. We cannot ignore it, but we can influence it. We can use self image to our advantage. Here are seven tips on how to do this:

1. Decide who you want to be or how you want to be in any given situation or phase of life or for your entire life. You can create a new self image or reinvent it if you don't like the one you have. You can create a new habit of thinking about who you are. Ideally, this is most productive when aligned with Your Soul and Your Person.

2. Visualize this new version of yourself. Be in this new person's skin and shoes. Imagine walking through the day. How will you interact with people? How will you feel in different situations? The more you can do this like an actor preparing for a new part, the better you

will feel when you start to do it in real life.

3. Act as if you are already the person you want to be. This technique, "Act As If," is simple and effective. Do things differently like the person you are striving to be. Think, act, speak, move, and react like your ideal persona. Make decisions from this place. Embody this right now! People and situations will start to change and react differently to you. The people you already know may take a while to buy into your change, but new people won't know the difference. Notice how they react and how your results start to change.

4. Surround yourself with supportive and like-minded people. It is difficult to master a new self image if everyone is still treating you like the old one. So let your support people know about the change, or join a new group that can support you. This is especially important if your people are the ones who helped create your initial Social Self. Yes, I am saying you may have to limit or separate yourself from your family or social group. Or if you can get them on board with your new efforts to change, they will often surprise you and can be super supportive, even your biggest fans.

5. Find a role model, someone you want to be like or someone who has a similar story to your dream. If they inspire you, emulate them or follow in their footsteps. Remember

we humans learn naturally by mimicking. A cautionary word here—remember you have your own unique journey to live and putting someone on an unrealistic pedestal can result in disappointments. Everyone is human and has struggled in life. So follow role models in moderation, while discovering your own path.

6. Notice when you slip back or get triggered into old unwanted patterns. This will happen. Notice, forgive yourself, learn, and get back to the new thinking. If these are areas that are true emotional wounds, be proactive and get professional help to heal these areas. This time and energy can be the greatest gift you could ever give yourself and the world you are trying to impact.

7. Stick to this new self image. Like all new habits, we need to practice, practice, and practice until new neuro-pathways are established, and the new habits form. That's how you achieve mastery.

Social Self Wrap Up

By now you have learned the impact your Social Self can have on you and your ability to live the extraordinary life that is possible for you. You have also learned that you can choose and change the rules you believe and how you see yourself. The key is to bring your subconscious autopilot thinking, reactions, and behaviors to your conscious awareness so you can start to understand and manage yourself differently.

This allows you to reprogram the values that govern your life. The new values then cascade into the meaning you give to different situations, how you speak to yourself, and how you see yourself and your capabilities. As a mentor coach of mine, Gretchen Pisano, says "Fire all of your thoughts and make them re-apply for the job!"

Do your thoughts, beliefs, and actions move you toward loving the world from your best self? From Your Soul? If not, you have the power, not to "Just Do It," but to just do "you" differently!

Part 4: Alignment

So how do we bring all the parts of the Trilogy together? How does your aligned Trilogy equal an extraordinary life?

If you remember, we talked about the three parts of you—your Soul, Your Person, and your Social Self—being like paper dolls. When they're out of alignment with each other, we're not happy—much less extraordinary. We are all askew, confused, and stuck in many ways.

You know by now that if you have been forcing your Soul and Person to align with your well-meaning but misguided Social Self, you will not be happy. Instead, you are living to please everyone else and in the process being stifled by your fear-based stories and beliefs.

You know that if you have been aligning to Your Person, your natural skills, and talents, you are getting closer to an extraordinary life. But if you rely only on your gifts and talents and you are ignoring your Divine Soul connection, you are limiting your extraordinary potential. Though you may be experiencing success in life, if it is not connected to your Soul's goal, you can still feel shallow and hollow inside because you are missing that connection.

Aligning your Trilogy with your Soul and its goals is really the key. Your Soul is already extraordinary; all you need to do to bring extraordinary into your life is to allow yourself to follow your Soul's guidance. To thrive and create a life that brings extraordinary results that matter to you and impact the world, you need to let your extraordinary self out. You do that by letting your Soul lead the other two parts. It is that easy and that challenging.

To find this sweet spot—where your spirit and talents and wisdom meet the needs of the world—you need to be diligent about connecting to your Soul messages. Make this connection your top priority and be willing to explore possibilities, decide on the best direction to follow, and then take action.

The *Goal* is to let your *Soul* out to *Play*.

Find what brings you meaning and joy and then follow that path. This is what it takes to be extraordinary. Take courageous action by letting yourself loose in the world to deliver your unique gifts and make your extraordinary impact on it.

The first step in this journey is Play.

Play is the Gateway to Extraordinary

Why Play? Because letting your Soul out to play opens the door to adventure and magic connecting you with warmth, love, and fun. This is the sweet spot, the gateway to extraordinary.

As strange as this may sound after all this serious introspection and the journey into self-understanding, play is all you really need. Well, love is all you need, according to the Beatles, right? Right. But Play is love and learning in action. When you stay connected to what feels like meaningful play and allow that to direct you, it will take you down paths you never could have foreseen.

Think about when you were a kid, before you were school age. All you did was play. You were truly yourself before your Social Self got a stranglehold on you. You explored the world. You were curious to find things you liked, and then you spent time doing those things. You did them with joy, laughter, and no worries. You didn't take yourself so seriously and allowed yourself to be guided by what interested you and made you happy.

Embracing this feeling, this attitude of play gives you courage and a "what the hell" mindset, moving you past the fear and anxiety of the unknown. Playing takes the pressure off, allowing you to explore and have fun until you find things you like.

When you are playing, you are joyful. Remember what that feels like on your body compass. Putting yourself on a diet of joy and playfulness keeps you connected to your Soul. So start with an attitude of play and come back to it every time you lose your way. What feels like play to you?

Play… but isn't that irresponsible? It might seem so. But although this process is more abstract than many other life success models, it does work which makes it the most practical approach. As my coaching teacher and sage, Martha Beck, says, "One foot in practical and one foot in dreaming." You still need to pay the bills and raise your children, but with one eye, hand, and foot firmly exploring and open to possibilities.

Give Yourself Permission to Play

Only you can decide to go down this road where your truest self will lead. But often this is where we get stuck right out of the gate. Your Social Self will try to shut you down before you even get started. Literally, giving your Social Self permission to play, relax and learn is a crucial step for many people, especially if you have been driving yourself to relentlessly achieve goals without Your Soul's direction.

It helps to take baby steps to let your Social Self ease into this new way of being. Gaining success with baby steps is just like a child learning to walk. With each step you get stronger and more skilled until you are running. It is not a race though, and you can stop and take breaks. You will not master this journey all at once, but it will be a lot easier with play in your heart.

The Responsibility Paradox

Although we are talking about play, you are not a child anymore. You are 100% responsible for your life. The outcome and the results—great or lousy—are all yours. You are in charge, so take the wheel and drive. Stop blaming others and complaining about your life. Whenever you do this, you are giving your personal power away or dishonoring the precious gift of free will you were born with. You are turning your back on the extraordinary.

Here is the paradox though: you are co-creating your life with the Divine. This paradox is difficult for some people to grasp. You are in control, and yet you are not. Life happens. Sometimes bad things happen. Sometime horrendously bad things happen.

Sometimes challenges and obstacles get in your way, or things just don't happen the way you hope or want them to happen. Or sometimes a once in a lifetime chance comes along, or that dream comes true! How you respond to either is where your personal responsibility comes back into play. What you decide to learn or make a situation mean and how you take action is where you regain control.

Here is where things start to get interesting and

extraordinary. Start noticing what you can take responsibility for, what you can change or impact. What can only you create, love, or take care of?

Many people avoid responsibility, but this is where the treasure is. When you invest in yourself in a healthy loving way, you get paid in dividends, not just monetarily, but in others caring for you. Your talents and love start being noticed and returned. This will enrich your life beyond money.

So, when you get an idea or inspiration that can help others, when you can create a solution, or when you have the opportunity to say a kind word, take action! That inspiration is the Divine saying, "Over here! This needs your help!" Then watch for the feedback from the world. If the feedback is good, great! And if it is overwhelmingly good, "It wants to happen," meaning the Divine wants it to happen in a big way. You are on a red-hot track of the Hot & Cold game variety. You are on the road to winning, riding shotgun with the Divine!

Decide on the Direction

Since you are taking full responsibility, you need to decide which way to go. This is another point where people often get stuck. They never pick a direction. They never make a commitment because they think they have to be sure before getting started. It doesn't work that way. You have to start before you can be sure.

Confidence grows from action, even the smallest action. Clarity comes from experience.

Even if you start and realize this is not what you wanted you can always turn around and say "No, this is not for me." The great thing about that is now you know what you don't want. Now you can decide on another direction. It is the Hot & Cold game all over again. But at some point, you must make a final decision and stick with it.

Before making a decision, you want to tune in to all your Soul indicators: your body compass, your Soul quakes, your optimal experiences, and your Soul's goal. This will help you make a decision about something you want or wish for, something that feels compelling, and something that you desire.

Next, you'll want to set the intention to create it.

Setting Your Intention

An intention is making a big picture decision and then asking the Divine to help you get there. It's similar to prayer but with more responsibility on your part. For example, let's assume your intention is:

> "I want more positive, fun, and connected relationships."

Great start. Now you can get more specific.

> "I want more positive, fun, and connected relationships with people of my age who live in my town."

"Help me see and create the path to get there."

The final line is to invite the Divine for wisdom or foresight beyond what you can create or imagine on your own.

"I ask for this or something better that is beyond what I can imagine for myself."

The purpose of setting intentions is threefold:

- You gain clarity by stating what you want.
- You are tapping into your Divine partnership and asking for help or guidance.
- You are committing to creating it, by informing the Trilogy, "Okay gang, this is what we are doing, so get on board and let's make it happen!" Notice there is a definite commitment and determination here and that is critical.

Intentions can help with anything you truly want as well as when you aren't quite clear about what you want yet. For example:

- I intend to discover what I truly desire.
- I intend to discover which path and/or work would bring me the highest joy.
- I intend to discover the gifts I came here to share.

- I intend to discover the life I would love to live.

It helps to write intentions down and read them daily or weekly to keep you focused. Some clients write them on note cards and read them when they get up in the morning and again before they go to sleep at night. Intentions can be adjusted as you get more clarity or your direction shifts. You own these dreams. Make them work for you.

Create a Plan of Action

Once you have set your intention and asked for help, it is time to create a plan. Even though this may feel counter to the magical nature of dreams, dreams love a step-by-step plan or a system. Create a plan even if it is a simple plan that outlines trying out various baby steps to see what happens. The better thought out the plan, the more likely your intention is going to become reality, so taking time to plan is critical. Things to consider in your plan include the following:

- Time
- Money
- Skills
- Moral support and help

Start by asking, "Who? What? When? Why? Where? and How?"

In coaching, we work through many different types of personalized action plans based on Your Person, how you naturally work best, and where you need the most support. So create a plan that works for you and don't be shy about asking for help. Just because it is your dream does not mean you have to do it alone.

A note about planning: Be open to adjustments. Things often do not go as planned, so being able to adjust and problem solve is crucial.

Courageous Action

Finally, it is "go" time. You can have all the greatest intentions, but nothing happens without action. This is the part that inspires people or can intimidate them. Being courageous and bold is necessary because you are now breaking norms in real life, not just in your thinking. In some ways, this will always feel counterintuitive to your survival instincts because it is risky and different from what you have known in the past. But fortunately, we are also built for action, for challenge, and to overcome obstacles.

New research confirms this paradox: people are at their happiest when they are working through a challenge, especially when they start to see that the effort is worth the reward.

When we take positive risk and gain positive rewards, we grow our confidence. We can also grow our confidence when we face adversity and learn from it. Sometimes the confidence comes just because we survived. So taking action is a win regardless of whether we succeed or fail.

When you take action aligned with your Soul, Your Person, and your supportive Social Self, especially inspired action, you will start to see the results both through more meaning and in increased productivity. Things will start to click and start happening with ease and serendipity. Like-minded people and friends who want to be a part of what you're doing will come into your life. This is when you know you are on to something. When you are aligned like this, it is like a compass pointing you in a clear direction. "This is the way." You will start gaining momentum. It will still be work, but it will feel more like play than any other work ever did.

The path may not always be direct because there are lessons to learn along the way. Remember, part of the Soul's goal is to teach you how to love more fully from your essence, and these lessons are best learned through setbacks. But one success will lead to the next and to the next until you learn to trust yourself and this way of living.

Determination and perseverance are critical when you are connected to your Soul's goal. You know you are connected when you have energy and passion for what you are doing. Yes, there will be hard days, days when you would rather quit. On these days, rest and play and ask yourself if your goal still lights you up? Does it still feel hot? Does it make you feel alive?

If the answer is "Yes," do not give up.

When Nothing Happens

If you feel passion for your purpose but things are not happening and momentum eludes you, there are many possible reasons:

1. You are somehow sabotaging your intention with Social Self issues. Examine your beliefs around your ability to be successful. Are your behaviors opposite to what you are trying to achieve?

2. You are trying to make something happen, and God has a bigger and better plan for you. This is a hard one but have faith, that there is something better coming your way. And keep praying, "For this or something better."

3. Sometimes you are just hesitating because you are not ready. This can be intuition, a Soul message. Maybe you need to let something go, or you are not finished with another assignment, or again, something better is coming.

4. You have missed a step or are out of alignment with your Trilogy. This often happens when we think we are better at things than we really are. Think *American Idol* tryouts when the contestants know they want to be on the show, but just don't have the skills or

need to refine their skills to be successful. What have you missed or what can't you see? Ask an honest, caring friend for insight.

5. You are pushing your goal too hard. This desperation will cause dreams to elude you because you want them in your own time, not in God's time. This demanding drives success further away. Stay connected to God's time, to what wants to happen, and to your Soul's messages. Playing with creative solutions will allow things to happen at the "right" time.

There is an art to knowing when to stay determined and when to let go. Letting go or putting things on hold, although counterintuitive, often gives us the answers we need. Reminding yourself you are not really in control is a test in humility, patience, and faith. There are infinite roads to your Soul's goal. The Divine knows the best route.

This final thought on courageous action: when you take action, the boundaries of what you believe about yourself and what is possible expand, so be bold and courageous because the bolder and bigger the possibility, the greater the impact, the more extraordinary. Someone is going to do it, why not you?

Be Devoted to Love

Love is a central theme in this book. Remember to return to it again and again whenever life takes you off course, as it will. Love starts with being connected to the Divine and giving self-compassion, patience, kindness, and service to yourself and to others. Remember the Divine can just mean being loving, positive, and kind—the reasons "why" you do anything. Notice the magic in the simplest things and be in awe of their magnificence. Let this remind you of your natural magnificence and the magic you are capable of bringing to the world.

Be grateful for all of life's gifts especially your own, even when you cannot fathom what part they play in the larger scheme of things. Have faith in love. It has faith in you.

From one ordinary human to another—may your life be filled with extraordinary blessings of your own Divine making!

Conclusion

As you move through the process of aligning your Soul, Your Person, and your Social Self, I hope you reach out to me with progress reports or questions. I'm available to help you in many ways, including through private coaching and group programs.

Here are the ways you can connect with me:

Website: www.zealcoach.com

Facebook: www.facebook.com/ZealCoaching

Bonus Workbook

The questions asked throughout the book have been gathered into a downloadable workbook for your use. Get your copy here:

www.zealcoach.com/ordinary-to-extraordinary

Recommended Tools:

StrengthFinders 2.0 by Tom Rath

Myers-Briggs Type Indicator (MBTI)

Strong Interest Inventory (SII)

Thank you

I hope you have enjoyed *An Ordinary Girl's Guide to Extraordinary*. Thank you from the bottom of my heart for reading this book. Writing it was a labor of love and I appreciate your time and attention to the results.

If so inclined, please take a few moments to write a review on Amazon and share your opinion with future readers. You can find the link in your purchase confirmation email, or search Amazon books for the title.

This book is also available on Kindle and other devices, so you can have an electronic copy for your convenience.

Acknowledgments

For nearly 4 decades I have been hooked on self-development. From the first books I read—*Love* by Leo Buscaglia and *Jonathan Livingston Seagull* by Richard Bach. So, it is hard to pinpoint where the wisdom and philosophy that emerged in this book originated.

I do know where they took root and flourished during the last decade though. Although I was already a coach, my Soul definitely altered with Oprah Radio's year of studying The Course in Miracles with Marianne Williams. The depth of this text and practice have helped me see love where there seemed to be none.

My life was further altered after reading two books and listening to one audio recording that clinched my resolve to study coaching with Martha Beck. Martha is a sage, genius, and mystic wrapped up in a Carol Burnette-like hilarious package. You have to love her. She and her tribe of coaches have nurtured, healed, inspired, stretched, and molded me into this extraordinary version of myself. Thank you specifically to Christina Brandt, Jennifer Voss, Renee Sievert, and Michele Woodward.

Add to that the collective wisdom and truth of the Bible, Mother Teresa, John Denver, Oprah Winfrey, Wayne Dyer, Elizabeth Lesser, Elizabeth Gilbert, Brené Brown, Daniel Pink, Byron Katie, Danielle LaPorte, Tony Robbins, Marie Forleo, Pam Grout, and Mike Dooley.

I do know my personal experimentation and mastery of this wisdom happened within my camp families and with the hundreds, maybe thousands, of clients at CYO Camp Rancho Framasa, my many YMCA camps, and Camp Joy in Clarksville, Ohio. These are the places that allowed me to first shine. Thank you! I would never have known who I could be without the love of my first Camp Family in the summer of 1986. You know who you are! Our hours of campfire and JD lives forever in my heart.

Then to my wealth of friends, I don't know how I got so lucky. From Indy to IU to Cinci to NB and now to Troy. You all, every single one of you, rock my world with love, support, and fun!!

Now to all my clients, who have allowed me to walk your journey with you for a long or short while. My heart does a crazy happy dance just to know you! Thank you for the honor. If you someday forget me, I will be the one with the pom-poms always cheering you on!

To Zach, my Intern Superman! Thank you for your friendship, love and dedication to all things Zeal!

Maryna Smuts you got me here, baby! From the first "you should write a book" suggestion to now with The Books Starts Here services. You and Sonya Myers have been miraculous with your know-how and the patience of angels. You two made this possible. It simply wouldn't have happened any other way.

To my family, ALL OF YOU, your unconditional love and acceptance is the foundation for my wonderful life. Jack, Patty, Rosie, Mary, Cathy, John, Jim, all your spouses, and all the kids. Plus Marilyn, Don, Rita, Ann, and Norm. I Love You!

Jason, Love you beyond measure. Runt!

Finally, to my true loves and the core of my heart: Stev, my rock; Monica, my jester; and Kyle, my muse. I love you more than all the drops of water and every blade of grass to infinity!!!

Made in the USA
Columbia, SC
23 September 2018